The Collaborative Imperative:
Librarians and Faculty Working Together in the Information Universe

Edited by

Dick Raspa
Wayne State University

Dane Ward
Central Michigan University

Association of College and Research Libraries
A division of the American Library Association
Chicago, 2000

The paper used in this publication meets the minimum requirements of American National Standard for Information Sciences–Permanence of Paper for Printed Library Materials, ANSI Z39.48—1992.∞

Library of Congress Cataloging-in-Publication Data
The collaborative imperative : librarians and faculty working together in the information universe / edited by Dick Raspa, Dane Ward.
    p. cm.
  Includes bibliographical references.
  ISBN 0-8389-8085-6 (alk. paper)
    1. Academic libraries--United States--Relations with faculty and curriculum. 2. Library orientation for college students--United States. I. Raspa, Richard, 1940- II. Ward, Dane.

Z675.U5 C6417 2000
027.7'0973--dc21

                                          00-028392

Printed in the United States of America.

03 04 02 01 00   5 4 3 2

Contents

Foreword

This project originated in 1996 from discussions within the Instruction for Educators Committee of ACRL's Education and Behavioral Sciences Section (EBSS). Originally, it was planned as an effort that would catalog current collaborative initiatives in higher education. But as it evolved, it also began to acquire some theoretical underpinnings and faculty perspectives that frequently were quite different from those held by librarians.

We want to acknowledge the support of many people. Pat Libutti provided guidance throughout our work on the book. As chair of EBSS, she was a strong advocate of librarian–faculty collaboration. In many ways, this book has grown out of her earlier EBSS initiatives. Patricia Senn Breivik initially brought us together to participate in the redesign of Wayne State University's freshman orientation course, and gave us the opportunity to present our work on collaboration and information literacy at the national conference of the American Association of Higher Education. Francine DeFranco and the EBSS Publications Committee provided encouragement and helpful feedback as our project progressed.

The members of the Instruction for Educators Committee have worked long and hard over the years attempting to define what this book would eventually become. Although some have since left the committee, these members have included: Susan Ariew, Sarah Beasley, Jean Caspers, Doug Cook, Bee Gallegos, Gail Gradowski, Shellie Jeffries, Katy Lenn, Carla Rosenquist-Buhler, Jennie Ver Steeg, Scott Walter, and Tom Wright.

Most especially, we are grateful for the support from our families: Dick's wife, Franziska, and daughter, Nikki; and Dane's wife, Jenny, and sons, Wil and Wesley. They offered solace when the terrain was rough, insight when the problems were Gordian knots, and ongoing encouragement when we could not see the project through to publication. They are our ever-present cheerleaders and our joy.

We hope you will find the contents of this book as valuable as we did in creating it. Collaboration will be the next great transition in higher education. We have a choice about how we will respond to it. We can either participate and experience new and life-enhancing possibilities, or we can let others define who and what we will become. This book offers tools for the choice to participate.

Dick Raspa
Dane Ward

December 1999

Introduction

This is a book about collaboration between librarians and faculty. It is a book about collaboration as it exists now and as it could exist in the future. We hope it will be a map for librarians and faculty to tomorrow's territory of higher education.

We, the editors of this book—one, a professor of humanities at Wayne State University, and the other, the coordinator of instruction services for the University Libraries at Central Michigan University—are two people who have collaborated for a number of years and pieces of our shared experience come out in several of the following essays. We have had a surprisingly similar feel for the interpersonal aspects of collaboration, which we consider to be the key to the entire process: the willingness to listen to each other. As becomes clear in these essays, working together without this interpersonal element is something other than collaboration. Perhaps, as Doug Cook writes, it is an attenuated form of networking or coordination.

During the past three years, this project has given us insights into our individual ways of working with others in higher education. It also has stretched us beyond our separate disciplines. We have learned how to work with each other, listening for ways to encourage ideas to flourish. Together, we have assessed this collection of essays from our integrated perspectives. Particularly when we differed about the merits of an essay, we sought to hear the other out, opening ourselves to take a second look at what we might have too quickly dismissed or too uncritically accepted. Perhaps we failed to see this or that insight in the piece, or maybe we missed a nuance here or there. Sometimes we had to confront a contributor and request extensive revisions. Collaboration made possible a second look at the essay, and in all instances, we believe, such second looks have improved the quality of the writing—our own as well as the others. Even more important has been the conversation we continue to have about how best to communicate the power of collaboration to you, the readers. Our intention is to persuade you, even nudge you, to risk engaging in the collaborative process at your institution. It is challenging work that repays with unexpected joy. To experience collaboration extends us beyond what we could have achieved on our own. The experience is powerful. As we march irrevocably toward a future world that is inflected on all levels by information technology, the major, perhaps even the dominant, mode of teaching and learning in higher education will require collaborative relationships.

Each chapter in this book explores the possibilities of librarians and faculty working together across disciplines and traditional university boundaries. In its own way, each essay encourages collaborative enterprises in the face of cynicism and resistance to change. The writings are premised on the observation that the world has changed. The paradigm has shifted. Globalization, information, and computer technology have inexorably altered the ways we read, research, write, and learn. Moreover, these changes have profoundly affected the way we do our work.

The following essays offer an opportunity to look carefully at this diamond called collaboration and to discover again and again the shining role that the act of listening plays in the development of relationships between librarians and instructional faculty. In the first essay, Dick Raspa and Dane Ward borrow from their shared experience to describe the interpersonal aspects of collaboration and, in particular, a special kind of listening that facilitates the process. Doug Cook's essay provides a state-of-the-art literature review of the topic, carefully delineating the differences among networking, coordination, and collaboration, with a variety of clarifying examples. In the next article, a group of librarians led by

Scott Walter and including Susan Ariew, Sarah Beasley, Mike Tillman, and Jennie Ver Steeg deliver five case studies of the listening that must take place at an institutional level to create powerful collaborative enterprises.

Raspa and Ward continue with an essay offering theoretical models from new work in the sciences that suggest ways for building collaboration. Bee Gallegos and Thomas Wright's text provides observations and summaries of twelve carefully selected surveys reporting on more informal collaborations. Shellie Jeffries's article reports on another survey about how librarians and faculty prefer to communicate with each other. Next, Dane Ward and Doug Cook's essay negotiates the rapids of change in the electronic environment by presenting us a "postmodern" directory of resources with specific Web sites and strategies for finding relevant information after the Web sites have disappeared. And finally, Jean Caspers and Katy Lenn's contribution looks into the future of collaboration and identifies a number of new conversations that will take place.

We know today that standard practices from the past do not suffice. They do not help much to deal with the complexities of contemporary life, nor with the realities of information. Old borders separating disciplines along departmental lines are blurring. The metaphor of knowledge as location—where matters pertaining to economics are housed in economics departments, those dealing with sociology in departments of sociology, and political issues confined to the department of political science—those easy partitions are crumbling. The old, fragmented view of disciplinary practice cannot deal with the complexity of social issues today. Understanding famine in third world countries, for example, is not merely a geologic or economic issue. Rather, it requires an interdisciplinary approach to get at the intertwining layers of geo-political, monetary, and cultural themes that give rise to the condition of famine, and that prevent adequate solutions from unfolding. Such understanding requires a number of competencies, including the power to analyze, synthesize, and present information in multiple contexts for very different audiences.

The big question is this: how can we deal with the ocean of information we find ourselves in? Can we intelligently navigate, or will we drown in it?

Listening for Collaboration: Faculty and Librarians Working Together

Dick Raspa
Wayne State University

Dane Ward
Central Michigan University

THE COLLABORATIVE VISION: THE BOND OF BELONGING, THE JOYFUL GIVE-AND-TAKE

> Interdependence joins us with others through the bond
> of a joyful give-and-take, a bond of belonging.... The
> bonds of interdependence are ties that set us free.
> —David Steindl-Rast

Collaboration is the bond of belonging. American philosopher David Steindl-Rast referred to the bond of belonging as interdependence, the joyful give-and-take that joins us with each other in enterprise. In collaboration, we are bonded to each other in acts of *listening* that endow enterprises with life and meaning. It requires hearing the other completely, waiting before speaking, recreating in one's mind what was just said, and making sure it was

1

understood. This way of listening holds judgment in suspension. Questions about being right or wrong yield to questions about ways of thinking and acting on behalf of the enterprise. Often, when we are engaged in solitary work, our critical faculty makes an assessment too quickly, before we have playfully elaborated an idea and given it the time and attention it deserves. Critical assessment of an embryonic idea is normally what aborts it before the idea is fully born. In collaboration, I give and take in the flow of conversation. I pull in this or release in that direction as I listen to you. You do the same for me. In that listening, enterprise is possible. We are joined together in a relationship that brings something to life.

Collaboration is useful to academics because of that special kind of listening. In higher education, such listening has the power to bring the enterprise of learning to life. Whether we like it or not, collaboration has become the educational imperative of the next century. Changes in our information universe, as well as advances in technology, require new ways of relating to each other in and out of the classroom. What is required is nothing less than breaking out of our boxes, reaching out to each other, and listening in this sense.

In the future, this type of collaboration between librarians and instructional faculty will be commonplace. Our work will include more partnerships and teams, each of us with a specialty, each blending individual work with that of others. As part of these teams, librarians and instructors will spend time together talking about ways to access, organize, and present information to classes and colleagues in a variety of textual and presentational forms: print, media, electronic, standard classrooms, as well as distance-learning formats, each with its special demands. Most of all, we will be challenged to listen to each other as collaborators. It is the listening that matters in collaboration.

In this chapter, the authors will define and develop this concept of collaboration, and discuss its importance in the future of higher education. In addition, they will talk about five personal qualities essential to the pursuit of collaborative relationships. These qualities enhance the type of interaction that is the hallmark of true collaboration. Ultimately, collaboration is a quality of interaction rather than a quantity of production, and can be identified more by the nature of relationship than by the shape of the organization. Our participation on committees and task forces does not ensure the existence of collaboration.

THE DEFINITION: COLLABORATION AS THE DIALOGUE OF WONDER

Technically speaking, collaboration may occur whenever two people work together. Both people bring their separate competencies to bear on a problem and work for a solution richer in options than might have been possible working alone. However, this definition fails to recognize the possibilities of interdependence. True collaboration is a working together through conscious acts of listening in which we recreate the other before we speak. Such listening acknowledges the potential for enterprise in the interplay between self and other. When we collaborate, we recognize that enterprise must be summoned in each other and focused in the world to be real. We work together to bring into being dreams that otherwise would lie dormant in the imaginations of separate people. Collaboration calls to life the energy and commitment to make something real.

Collaboration occurs in every domain of life. In marriage, it is the ability to stand together and face the world, or to stand apart and face each other. Collaboration in marriage invites us to tell the truth, especially in moments of crisis, and at the same time to honor the other. In work life, collaboration is the ability to deal respectfully with conflict and yet align behind common goals. In education, collaboration is the ability to wonder together—to ponder the elegance of a quadratic equation, the intricacies of DNA, the blinding illuminations of a Goya painting. In the library, collaboration is the power of wonder as well, wondering with faculty and students how to explore a problem in the universe of information, a universe where everything radiates in fields of energy and light, and all boundaries separating domains are constructed by the human mind.

In the academic literature, *collaboration* is widely and loosely used to refer to situations in which two or more people work together to accomplish a task. Discussion about the quality or process of the relationship generally remains secondary to discussion of the resulting product. This neglect is surprising because strong interpersonal processes—where collaborators listen carefully to each other—are likely to yield much better results.

This nonspecific use of *collaboration* produces some confusion when we begin to make distinctions based on process. The term is frequently used synonymously with terms such as *networking* and *coordination*, which differ qualitatively in terms of interpersonal process, as well as quantitatively in terms of goals, methods, and outcomes. "Networking," according to A. T. Himmelman involves "exchanging information for mutual benefit," and represents an informal process with few, if any, clear goals or outcomes.[1] We network with each other at workshops, receptions, and campus restaurants, sharing news of interest to each of us.

Coordination suggests that individuals have identified a common goal but are working toward it independently, completing their parts of the process without any overlapping responsibility. This kind of working relationship remains common in the realm of library-related instruction: the faculty member and the librarian schedule a session that fits into the syllabus, and the librarian teaches a one-hour session on finding information in the subject area. In both networking and coordination, we find a lack of commitment to, or necessity of, a sustained interpersonal relationship or a more pervasive interdependence.

P. W. Mattessich and B. R. Monsey described collaboration as a "mutually beneficial and well-designed relationship entered into by two or more [individuals or] organizations to achieve common goals."[2] Key to this definition is an enterprise based on a relationship or connection that meets the needs of individuals and organizations. This definition adequately describes the external features of collaboration but fails to consider the interpersonal dimension. In addition to being a "well-designed" relationship, collaboration should be an integrated and authentically interpersonal relationship as well.

Unlike networking and coordination, collaboration is a more pervasive, long-term relationship in which participants recognize common goals and objectives, share more tasks, and participate in extensive planning and implementation. Collaborators share the give-and-take listening that creates the bond of belonging to a learning community. It is a more holistic experience in which we are committed to the enterprise, the relationship, and the process. We become indivisible, like the lake, the rain, and the banana leaf in this haiku:

> The Great Dance
> Down the Barley Rows
> Stitching, stitching them together
> The Butterfly goes.

> The Lake is Lost
> in the Rain which is lost
> in the Lake.
> Evening Rain,
> the Banana Leaf
> Speaks of it first.

Like the butterfly in the Haiku poem, "The Great Dance," we are connected to the earth around us, affecting it, touching it, reflecting it, in our simplest motions. We collaborate with the world whether we intend it or not. The butterfly and the growing barley, the rain and the lake, the rain and the banana leaf, are in a universal dance of belonging. Each of us is involved at all times in a dance with all the forms of life.

When we collaborate, we make visible that implicit bond between living entities. Particularly in human enterprises, collaboration is the special bond that calls forth something that would not easily be accessible in solitude. That something is a quality of listening that allows enterprise to show up, be entertained, be probed in a give-and-take fashion, and, finally, be borne into the public world of discourse and social action.

We marvel at the ways of figuring and configuring the world and its problems. To wonder this way is to draw out the other—our collaborator—and together ponder the mystery of things, provoking questions, more questions, and still more questions to be researched, and even, sometimes, to find an answer or two that satisfies the soul's yearning for meaning. Occasionally, collaboration inspires the rapture of insight. To collaborate with another is to venture behind the polite fences that categorize the world and keep us, for the time being, safe. To collaborate is to enter that liminal space where we do not know the answer beforehand, but we see, feel, and sense the traces of some phenomenon, and most important, are willing to have our safe formulations, our fictions of order, our walls protecting us from chaos, disrupted and even torn apart.

In higher education, collaboration is the passionate pursuit of knowledge in dialogue, in the joyful give-and-take of intelligent listening where we hear the other and are heard by him or her. On the journey into knowing, sometimes we may feel as though we are being pushed and shoved, and in those moments we need to remind ourselves to stay open to the other as partner and fellow traveler. In this collaborative process we risk the past, the old questions, the antiquated solutions, we even risk who we are and what we believe is true, real, and good. Collaboration poises us to encounter the other in the dialogue of wonder and, together, to enter the search for meaning and truth. Collaboration is not just a way of thinking and acting; rather, it is a mode of being, a way of being with the other. To work with—to collaborate—is to be with each other in states of wonder and to find ourselves in states of belonging.

Librarians are particularly suited for collaborative enterprise. They practice daily the kind of listening that requires them to translate for students and instructional faculty the questions they bring to the library. Librarians are on the edges of research, on the first threshold where the researcher has an idea or a hunch about something but needs a guide to navigate the waters of inquiry. Librarians know issues change shape, even vanish, depending on where the inquirer situates him- or herself in the search process. The librarian is there at the beginning, like Virgil in Dante's journey, to point the way through the labyrinthian channels of information.

THE PRACTICE: LISTENING FOR THE JOY

Successful collaboration requires sustenance from the participants. It cannot be mandated or assumed. It cannot be undertaken unilaterally or coaxed into existence. By nature, collaboration is a fragile relationship possibly destined for great achievements. But powerful collaboration requires significant effort, lots of time, and a desire to make things happen. Above all else, it requires space for listening: listening to our self and to the "other." It requires space for exploration without the pressure of immediate result. Good results will come, but they will come later.

Today's working environment is more fluid, less individualistic. In it, we are able to initiate a period of "wondering together" in which we define issues of common concern and agree to work together, not necessarily to find quick and simple answers but, rather, to participate in an open-ended process of dialogue and exploration. Listening is the only thing that continues, like an undercurrent. If the participants can break into collaboration, they learn to live in the question. In other words, they look at the question from different perspectives, holding all perspectives before settling into the one that satisfies. Over time, collaborators may experience more complex and powerful conceptualizations that evolve from the joyful give-and-take of listening.

Collaboration may be divided into formal and informal varieties. On an informal, more personal level, we may undertake a collaborative enterprise with a friend or colleague who has a similar interest. Perhaps a social work librarian and a faculty member decide to apply for a grant that integrates information skills and technologies into an undergraduate course. If successful, it may attract attention and serve as a model for the entire school. On a formal, organizational level, collaborative projects may be created by or between departments, colleges, or schools. In either case, there needs to be a wide-ranging commitment, not only among the departments, but also among the individuals.

Five fundamental qualities are required for collaboration: passion, persistence, playfulness, promotion, and project. Taken together, the "Five Ps of Collaboration" represent a way of activity that grows out of our engaged listening to the other and to the self. Organizationally, they point to a way of enlisting others in discussion that leads to making things happen. In order for collaboration to take place, you will need:

Passion: What is your passion, your joy? What are your skills? What might you bring to the enterprise? On the one hand, many librarians with a background in education will be interested in collaborative efforts to develop powerful classroom experiences. Those with strong subject expertise may want to conduct research with faculty colleagues. On the other hand, instructional faculty may be interested in exploring active teaching methods with library resources or may take a personal interest in collection development policies that support the curriculum. Of course, technology represents an area of overlapping interest. It is important, in any event, to take on projects whose requirements match your abilities and interests. You will find little happiness in a project for which you are not suited, or one that does not grow out of your joy.

Persistence: Are you willing to persist in the face of opposition—subtle and clear—from colleagues, institutional structures and/or administrative inertia? Other questions: do you have the desire and commitment to find others with whom you can talk and collaborate? Our circumstances are all different, but it is clear that finding and working with partners in the university can be a difficult experience. Our institutions are typically not organized to promote collaboration beyond our disciplines. In the absence of formal institutional initiatives, you will have to set them up on your own. You need to take every opportunity to promote collaboration. Begin now. Open the conversation with one other person in your department. Then invite one or more faculty members to attend a demonstration of library resources or a session you or another department member will present on research. There is risk, of course. You may get a few no-thank-yous along the way, but you will eventually get positive responses and enjoy an abundant harvest.

Playfulness: Are you willing to play? Being playful does not mean not taking work seriously or trivializing our enterprise. Rather, playfulness is the capacity to engage an enterprise deeply—mind, heart, and spirit—all parts of us brought into the action of the moment. To engage the world playfully is to be passionately engaged in the here and now, focused on what is right before us. It is a wholly satisfying experience; it is what Mihaly Csikszentmihalyi calls "flow" and what Abraham Maslow calls "peak experience."[3,4] It is that moment when we are at our best—relaxed, yet alert, poised for whatever shows up, ready to engage it without complaint or blame. To be playful is to be caught up in the action before us, and everything else—our fears, our concerns, our resentment and regret—fades into the background of consciousness and all that remains is the here and now. To get to the state of playfulness requires suspending what you already know about those people you work with and approaching the others as someone new. You create possibilities when we can release the past and focus on the present. In contrast, the person who already "knows" how another person thinks or behaves kills the relationship. To collaborate in the invention of something new requires the "not knowing/ listening" that opens us to possibilities. If we can pretend that the question before us—the one that this student or that instructor has—is the most important in the world at that moment, we can play.

Project: Are you willing to take on a big project? Collaboration must revolve around a focus, a project to which participants may contribute their ideas and energies. Consider some of the great collaborations: the Wright brothers and the problem of flight, the Manhattan Project and nuclear weapons, Disney and animated cartoons. All had a specific project, and the participants had a personal commitment to that project. Warren Bennis and Patricia Ward Biederman wrote that great teams feel they are on a mission from God.[5] Great expectations inspire grand outcomes.

Promote: Are you willing to talk about your passion and projects around your institution? Recognizing that collaboration is really an issue of building relationships, we encourage institutions, departments, and individuals to undertake initiatives that enhance internal and external communication. An atmosphere of openness to individual differences is critical to the development of collaboration. The authors strongly advocate the use of personality tools such as the Myers-Briggs Type Indicator (MBTI) to help individuals understand the diversity of work styles in their environment and to work with them more effectively. The authors have found a marvelous collaborative experience in working with those of similar, but not identical, personality type, although this would not necessarily be the same for everyone. In many cases, opposite types complement each other.

When all "Five Ps of Collaboration"—passion, persistence, playfulness, project, and promotion—are present, collaboration is a likely possibility. The authors suggest beginning in groups of two or three and gradually expanding the circle. Begin at lunch or during a break. There is no right time to begin. It may be as simple as engaging the people right before you, such as the instructor who comes to the library for instruction on the computers or the librarian who expresses interest in your research. In that moment, your listening as a librarian or instructor is on display. You have the opportunity to demonstrate to colleagues how to listen and participate in their ongoing research projects.

Librarians have the ability to guide users through a search procedure, from location to collaboration. What is required is the librarian stretching and taking the first step. Many instructional faculty underestimate the power of librarians, who in fact have the opportunity to begin to shift that way of thinking and invite a deeper listening to the problem. Librarians can show, for example, how asking different questions produces different results. And how inventing new ways of looking at topics produces different searches. As you read these suggestions, you probably will notice that what the authors are suggesting is a classical rhetorical approach to research—Aristotle in virtually pure form. The researcher invents the topic in the questions he or she asks, invents his audience or readers or listeners, and shapes and organizes the material to suit his purpose and audience. Librarians collaborate with the instructor and the students, and all of us collaborate with the print or electronic sources we are retrieving. Everyone is listening to everyone else, and in the give-and-take of that belonging—belonging to this class, this group, this community of researchers exploring this or that topic, and finally participating in this universe of discourse known as the university. It is in listening that we come to belong, and it is up to us to extend our listening to others. If we wait for others to invite us, we may be waiting a long time to enter the dance.

Of course, instructional faculty share equal responsibility for initiating collaborative endeavors. By inviting librarians to participate in their research or their classroom instruction, they can take the first critical step toward growing a community of learners and listeners. Through a process of careful listening, faculty can discover the formal and informal parameters within which individual librarians work, and can learn the willingness of potential colleagues to engage with them in a pursuit of research and belonging. Numerous issues may prevent us from working together in a meaningful way, but without asking, we will never take that first step on the floor.

A Case Study: Three Phases of Collaborative Wonderment

The authors see three phases in the growth and development of a collaborative enterprise: (1) collegial, (2) interpersonal, and (3) syncretic. Phase one is the initial stage when the two partners stay in their own domains and work from the conventions of their own disciplines. Over the past three years, the authors have engaged in a collaborative relationship. Initially, they met as members of a team gathered to redesign UGE 1000, Wayne State University's freshman orientation course, which Raspa had directed and taught for four years. During this introductory phase, the two potential collaborators worked within the context of a large, formally organized working committee that provided limited opportunities for interpersonal discussion. Nevertheless, even in this group, Raspa (from the Interdisciplinary Studies Program) and Ward (from the

University Libraries) began to recognize common interests in, if not approaches to, life and teaching.

"Dick was fascinating," says Ward. "His concern for students and his passion for authentic communication in the classroom captured everyone's imagination. I knew intuitively during those meetings that he and I had a lot in common."

Raspa comments: "Every time I saw Dane at the library, he asked me what I was researching. And he always tried to connect to that. Dane has an uncommon sense of wonder about the world. Research is an exquisite form of play for him, and he delights in dancing around, inside, forward, and then back and through a topic—not alone in the solitary precincts of the self, but out there, out here, on the floor of the library. There is no perfect moment for connecting with another human being. There will always be problems going on, always things to do, always the feeling of being pulled in five different directions at once, and never enough time. Dane gave the time that was necessary to establish a relationship, and he did it by simply taking the risk of listening."

In phase two, the partners begin to explore both personal and interdisciplinary areas of interest, and may undertake small projects. They take an interest in understanding aspects of the other field and attempt to incorporate ideas and concepts from that field into their own. They listen to each other in the collaborative sense discussed in this essay. A commitment begins to grow, and they move toward common goals within an interdisciplinary language. In the context of librarian–faculty collaboration, these goals may have something to do with incorporating information skills and technologies into the curriculum using active teaching methods. For the authors, this phase resulted in several clearly defined, short-term projects in which they participated in the continuing evolution of UGE 1000. This dialogue led further afield into areas such as new information technologies, models of teaching, and student learning. Finally, the authors began to share more about their interests, work, and families.

"Some of our discussions during this phase were eye-opening experiences for me," says Ward. "I found great power in Dick's use of metaphors to describe learning in higher education, and in life. He has a unique way of providing meaningful contexts for understanding ideas and developing them with a student or colleague so that together, we leap to a greater understanding with a capital *u*. Naturally, my job as a librarian has required me to be pretty pragmatic in my planning and decision making. But that doesn't mean I am unable to participate in the great adventure of learning at our institution. In fact, once Dick and I began teaching and working together, the possibilities seemed limitless."

Raspa says: "Dane is instantly curious. He sees everything connected to everything else and marvels at the associations. This capacity to marvel he brings to the library and to the classroom. Students feel validated by having their ideas taken seriously. So our conversations ranged over many fields."

In the end, the authors contributed a structural change to UGE 1000, which reaches about 2,400 students each year. In each section of this seven-week class, students meet for two weeks in the new Adamany Undergraduate Library, where they create a strategy for finding information, find full-text articles in the computers, and explore critical thinking within the growing information universe. As reconfigured, the course focuses on teaching and learning the research process and incorporates the potential for greater interaction—if not collaboration—among instructors, librarians, and students.

In phase three, the boundaries separating the disciplines begin to blur, and the partners are in the space of collaboration, or of listening together in this special way. The partners find a language and common goals. The authors took advantage of this synergistic opportunity to work together teaching the course, and rapidly discovered similar beliefs about the importance of engaging students through meaningful discussion, humor, and interactive sessions. Their collaboration in this phase yielded an infectious classroom atmosphere characterized by student interest, playfulness, and a passion for learning.

The collaborators found common interests in areas such as Csziksentmihalyi's "flow theory," the Myers-Briggs Type Indicator, and Parker J. Palmer's writings on the power of teaching and community in higher education.[6] A remarkable similarity in personality type reinforced their recognition of mutual understanding and laid the foundation for work on other projects, including presentations on their collaborative experience at two national conferences. One paper, discussing the importance of collaboration in teaching and learning information literacy, resulted from a brief two days of collaborative writing.

This experience suggests that collaborative relationships may continue growing indefinitely. Rather than diminishing in any way, the author's ability to share and play with creative ideas continued to grow in phase three, as did the epiphanies resulting from a continued "wondering together."

"Back at Wayne State," Ward says, "we continued to work together teaching sections of the orientation course, organizing presentations, writing articles, and envisioning future projects."

The UGE 1000 course continues to be refined, and together the authors continue to invent ways students can engage the research process—searching for information, analyzing and organizing it, and then presenting it.

"And beyond the boundaries of the university, we continued to explore the parameters of our collaboration. Not surprisingly, it spilled over into other aspects of our lives. For instance, our families met and enjoyed each other immensely."

This extended family relationship grew to include even more pervasive, unexpected, and magical forms of collaboration. "During the Christmas holidays, my wife telephoned Dick to ask if he could recommend a book that she could buy for me. Because I'm a librarian, it's very difficult for people to choose new books for me to read. But Dick chose the perfect book." That book by David Steindl-Rast contains the quote on interdependence that begins this essay.

Collaboration should be a natural part of life, pursued in the name of personal and organizational growth. Ultimately, it is about relationship, and requires fresh air and water to grow to discover its potentials and possibilities. Collaboration should be a celebration of the relationship.

Listening and Belonging: The Future of Higher Education

As we speed into the new millenium, librarians and instructional faculty will continue exploring new ways of working and listening together. The best examples of working together will incorporate models of listening together. Effective teaching and learning in this increasingly interdisciplinary environment will require us to share carefully and not to assume that we know what the other person means. The new information universe will require nothing less. We must shift our thinking about being independent teachers and learners to adapt to the needs of this shape-shifting environment. It will be a world where change is the constant and flux is the norm, where novel instructional pairings and collaborations between members of the academic community will be commonplace. At best, our current conceptions of teaching and learning represent a transitional phase in a grand movement toward a new form of higher education characterized by changing places, departments, teams, and subjects. In the new university, librarians and instructors will come together in constantly moving venues that will require patience, flexibility, and skills in that special form of "not knowing/listening" that the authors consider the hallmark of collaboration.

During this transitional phase, we will begin working with those forms of organizational relationships to which we have become accustomed, but gradually we will reach out to—or perhaps be reached by—colleagues interested in the same kinds of interpersonal and interprofessional growth. The future of learning will require us to step out of those boxes or departments within which we work. This transformational period will demand Herculean efforts to redefine who we are, what we do, and how we work.

Several trends will continue to move us toward true collaboration. First, this increasingly complex and expansive information universe makes it impossible for individuals to master all of the relevant interdisciplinary subject content and skills. In the instructional arena, we have reached a point at which neither librarians nor instructional faculty can adequately teach the research process in isolation from each other. Librarians do not have the subject expertise required in teaching in the disciplines. Instructional faculty are not knowledgeable about the changes occurring on a daily and weekly basis in our exploding information universe. It takes both classroom instructors and librarians to teach students to develop adequate research skills.

Second, with increased demands for instructional accountability, we are experiencing pressures to explore alternative, more effective ways of teaching and learning. Here, we are turning more frequently to active teaching methods, such as resource-based learning, which in best case scenarios involves collaboration among instructors, librarians, and students.

In their own instructional collaboration, the authors have carefully planned out their philosophy and approach to UGE 1000, which stress "engagement" and immediacy. Both of them strive to overcome the traditional barriers separating themselves from students and each other. Students conduct research on the library's computers for full-text articles providing information that will help their team in a final debate on a topic such as "should euthanasia be banned in Michigan."The authors make special efforts to engage these hesitant freshmen with their peers in discussing specific arguments and to give technical support where needed. But as in any resource-based learning activity, students learn by doing.

Third, in this postmodern era, employees will seek more personal satisfaction from their work in the university. The old monetary rewards may not be enough in the next century; librarians and instructional faculty will look for rewards in the various interpersonal processes of their work environment. Collaboration may be one of these. We spend about one-third of our lives in the workplace. It is clear that in the future, employees will demand work processes, such as collaboration, that enhance their lives.

The fourth trend that will facilitate more collaborative enterprises has to do with discussions about our future within academe itself. The reformation of higher education is taking place in discussions on an interdisciplinary level. Our academic boxes keep us from seeing the big picture, keep us from participating in the broader discussions now taking place on our campuses. If we feel passionately about the importance of libraries and information skills in the future of higher education, it is our responsibility to take action. If we wait for the future, we may not be part of it. But through collaboration, we can participate in shaping the world.

THE INTERPERSONAL INSPIRATION TO MOVE AHEAD

Key to the success of any collaborative enterprise will be our ability to listen to each other patiently and without assuming we know what the other person is saying or thinking. This means slowing down and not jumping to conclusions; it means focusing on the interpersonal aspects of the interactive process. As a Peace Corps Volunteer in Senegal, West Africa, one of the authors (Ward) learned long ago the importance of building relationships before building bridges. Although we may be tempted to follow a very logical and linear path for completing tasks and solving problems, other cultures stress more relational processes. In Senegal, it is important for everyone to participate and be heard; through this process, each person seeks a personal way to feel good about the task.

In addition, we must live and practice the Five Ps of Collaboration: always pursuing our passion and persevering in promoting our project, but never forgetting to play. Our collaborative efforts must find sustenance in personal meaning and inspiration; without it, our work becomes a series of disembodied tasks in which other people are mere objects or talking heads. We must find the authenticity within ourselves in order to listen authentically to others. And we will find that authenticity in that which inspires us.

No matter how precisely—or not—we use the term *collaboration*, it is important to remember that whenever we work with others, our best results will come from the process of "not knowing/listening." In the end, building relationships allows us to build stronger bridges.

CONCLUSION

In this chapter, the authors have defined collaboration as a special form of listening that comes from attending to the relationship behind the project. They have described the growth of their own special working relationship and identified five elements they consider critical to the pursuit of collaboration. Finally, the authors have speculated about the changes in higher education that will impact librarian–faculty working relationships.

NOTES

1. A.T. Himmelman, "On the Theory and Practice of Transformational Collaboration: From Social Service to Social Justice," in *Creating Collaborative Advantage*, ed. C. Huxham (London: Sage, 1996), 27.

2. P. W. Mattessich and B.R. Monsey, *Collaboration: What Makes It Work* (St. Paul, Minn.: Amherst H. Wilder Foundation, 1992), 7.

3. See, for example, Mihaly Csikszentmihalyi, *Flow: the Psychology of Optimal Experience* (New York: Harper & Row, 1990).

4. See, for example, Abraham Maslow, *Religions, Values, and Peak-Experiences* (New York: Penguin, 1964).

5. Warren Bennis and Patricia Ward Biederman, *Organizing Genius: The Secrets of Creative Collaboration* (Reading, Mass.: Addison-Wesley, 1997).

6. See, for example, Parker J. Palmer, "Good Teaching: A Matter of Living the Mystery," *Change* (Jan./Feb. 1990): 11–16; ———, "Divided No More: A Movement Approach to Educational Reform," *Change* (Mar./Apr. 1992): 10–17; ———, "Good Talk about Good Teaching: Improving Teaching through Conversation and Community," *Change* (Nov./Dec. 1993): 8–13; ———, *The Courage to Teach: Exploring the Inner Landscape of a Teacher's Life* (San Francisco: Jossey-Bass, 1998).

Creating Connections:
A Review of the Literature

Doug Cook
Shippensburg University

Alliance, partnership, networking, relationship, teamwork, collaboration, coordination, cooperation, liaison, building bridges— no matter what you call it, these words describe creating connections with the rest of the campus community.

During this decade of current emphasis on information literacy and rapid technological change, librarians have been forced to rethink their role in academia. In the past, they have often been characterized by a passive "keeper of the books" mentality. Recently, however, academic librarians have taken a more active partnership role in the education of college students.

One of the tremendously positive results of this recent role shift has been the connections that have been created between the library and the rest of the campus. This chapter summarizes a recent literature search regarding these connections. In years past, libraries were often given lip service as the "heart of the campus," but in actuality they never really seemed to be as central as that platitude seemed to indicate. But because librarians of the 1990s have begun to take a more proactive role, that worn-out "heart of the campus" cliché seems closer to the truth.

A recent search of the library literature for articles on the topic of library–campus connections met with mixed results, which fall into two major categories. The vast bulk of these recent articles are of the "how-we-done-it-good" variety. In fact, this search revealed more than 400 articles of this type. Academic librarians have created liaison programs, given workshops, set up elaborate information literacy programs, become experts at browsing the World Wide Web, etc.—all in the process of connecting to the rest of the academic community. In fact, there are so many of these articles that it is impossible to detail them all in the scope of this essay.

The second major category of articles from the library literature related to making connections spoke to the reasons and need for making connections. Far, far fewer of these articles exist. Most of them are editorials that call for librarians to reach outside the walls of the library to create connections with the rest of the college community.

In preparing to write this essay, it became necessary to go outside the library literature to look at and define methods for creating connections. The literature of the social sciences was sampled to discover definitions of various types of connections and to outline some basic components of collaboration.

Therefore, this essay highlights three areas. First, it explores the current academic climate and the need for librarians to make connections. Second, it establishes a definition of collaboration and examines various types of cooperative efforts. Third, it attempts a recapitulation of the many ways that librarians are currently making connections. Rather than discussing each of these 400 plus articles, categories are established and representative articles discussed.

PART ONE: THE BASIS FOR MAKING CONNECTIONS: A PROACTIVE ROLE FOR ACADEMIC LIBRARIANS

A review of this literature resulted in two facets of the current climate in academia that make it vital for librarians to make connections to the rest of the academic community. First, the rapid technological changes that have occurred in the past thirty years in the way that information is stored and accessed has radically changed the way librarians do business. Second, the rise of information literacy as the primary focus of the teaching library has created an environment that is ripe for collaboration.

Technological innovation occurs again and again as a driving theme in these articles. Computerization and digitalization—more than anything else in the history of academic librarianship—has forced librarians to redefine their roles.

Information Explosion

The vast quantity of information available on almost any subject can be absolutely staggering to an undergraduate attempting to do research. Often classroom faculty themselves have a difficult time keeping up with the very latest occurrences in their fields due to the sheer rapidity with which they occur.[1]

Not only has the amount of information available increased, but also the methodology by which this information is accessed has changed. Faculty members who have found it very comfortable to do library research using a card catalog and paper indexes need to learn new skills to become effective searchers in today's electronic environment.[2] With the advent of computerized indexing and digital storage, the discovery and retrieval of information has become much more efficient. However, electronic databases cannot be searched using the same skills learned to search the card catalog.

It has become the livelihood of academic librarians to stay abreast of the techniques and strategies of electronic searching. Because they are the first to interface with these databases (often before they have been released for public use), librarians have indeed become the campus experts on modern electronic research methodology. Academic librarians currently have skills that classroom faculty may not have had a chance to learn.

According to J. Young these rapid changes have presented an ideal opportunity for librarians to create connections with faculty colleagues.[3] Not only can librarians help faculty learn new research strategies and techniques, but they can also assist faculty with the creation of effective research assignments for their students.

The Rise of Information Literacy

The rise of information literacy as a driving force behind the modern academic library has made it necessary for librarians to create connections. Information literacy has "enjoyed a rapid, almost whirlwind period of development and growth" during the past three decades.[4] In fact, information literacy has come to be viewed as the basis of academic library service. G. Fernandez wrote that "bibliographic education must be seen as a basic goal of librarianship."[5]

One of the clearest models with which to understand the implementation of instruction as a major goal of the library is that of the "teaching library."[6] A teaching library can be defined as one that is "actively and directly involved in advancing all aspects of the mission" of the academic institution.[7] Librarians in the teaching library are not passive "warehouse managers" but, instead, are active "partners who have considerable resources and expertise to contribute to the teaching, service, and research missions of the institution."[8] The core component of the teaching library is a comprehensive bibliographic instruction program.

It is generally recognized that the most effective way to provide students with the information-seeking skills they will need to achieve information literacy should be provided in course-integrated library instruction. Fernandez has called this instructional partnership between librarians and faculty the "ideal approach for promoting the utilization of library resources and the development of critical skills in information use."[9] Library instruction of this type provides ample opportunity for librarians to create connections with their faculty colleagues. In reality, if these lines of connection are not cemented, the teaching library will cease to exist. A teaching library is a proactive library with a multitude of connections to the rest of the academic community.

Because of recent technological changes and validation of the teaching library model, librarians are playing a more active role in the campus community. The opportunity is here for librarians to create connections with the campus. Part two of this essay provides some theoretical basis for how such connections can be created.

PART TWO: MODELS FOR MAKING CONNECTIONS

This section reviews the theoretical literature of the social sciences that sheds light on creating connections. First, a definition of the most complex type of alliance—collaboration—is established. Also the components of successful collaboration are discussed. Second, two other types of relationships—networking and coordination—are compared and contrasted with collaboration. In each case, an example from the library literature is used to further explain these theoretical concepts.

Definition and Components of Collaboration

A number of articles have been written that study a more formal type of connection commonly called "collaboration." Studying a formalized effort to make an alliance can give valuable insight into how to go about such an undertaking.

P. W. Mattessich and B. R. Monsey have devised a basic working definition of collaboration: "Collaboration is a mutually beneficial and well-designed relationship entered into by two or more [individuals or] organizations to achieve common goals."[10] According to this definition and others in the literature, collaboration has three basic components:

1. Collaboration's purpose is to "achieve common goals."
2. Collaboration is supported by a "well-designed" structure.
3. Collaboration is "mutually beneficial."

The Sharing of Mutual Goals

D. G. Appley and A. E. Winder,[11] A. T. Himmelman,[12] and Mattessich and Monsey agree that one of the hallmarks of working together in a collaborative fashion is the sharing of mutual goals. This "shared vision" is often the starting point for beginning a collaborative effort. Mattessich and Monsey relate that shared vision stems from concentrating on a specific problem that needs to be solved.[13] Focusing on a common problem is a starting point for creating connections between librarians and the rest of the academic community.

Whether the problem is as complex as the need for a new library building or as sublime as the need to teach students that they cannot believe everything they see on the Web, these real-life dilemmas can become the basis for a cooperative effort between faculty and librarians. Thus, a shared vision can become the basis for library–faculty collaboration.

Creation of Common Structure

Appley and Winder and Mattessich and Monsey acknowledge that a common structure is needed for a collaborative effort to succeed.[14, 15] After a common problem is identified and several individuals decide to do something about it, a structure or a plan needs to be created. Mattessich and Monsey relate that at this point, a discussion of what is to be done to solve the problem and a discussion of the role each individual will play is especially valuable.[16] A collaborative team to deal with a complex issue such as the designing of a new library building may need a relatively complex and long-term planning structure to succeed. Many different constituencies would need to be represented. Many different types of needs would be considered. On the other hand, a collaborative effort to teach students to apply critical thinking skills when searching the Web would need a less complex structure. A librarian and a classroom faculty member could collaborate to create a series of assignments that would work toward solving this problem within the context of a particular course.

The Sharing of Mutual Benefit

Himmelman, Huxham, and Mattessich and Monsey have found that mutual benefit is a common component of collaboration.[17–19] This could be construed pragmatically as the solution to the shared problems that lead to collaboration. A discussion of how to solve a particular problem can go a long way toward shaping the nature of the collaborative effort that needs to be undertaken.

The solution to a need for a new library building is obviously a new building. The solution to the problem of students believing what they see on the Web may be the creation of a class assignment or a presentation. Oftentimes unexpected benefits, such as feelings of goodwill and collegiality, occur as a result of a collaborative effort.

An Example of the Components of Formal Collaboration: Designing an Internet Workshop

In a journal article titled "Designing and Implementing a Faculty Internet Workshop: A Collaborative Effort of Academic Computing Services and the University Library," Jane T. Bradford, coordinator of library instruction, Kelly E. Kannon, training coordinator for academic computing services, and Susan M. Ryan, government documents librarian, described a collaborative effort to train faculty members at Stetson University in the fine art of using the Internet.[20] The authors described a well-planned, three-day workshop designed to meet a need discovered via an assessment survey of the faculty. Colleagues from the computer center and the Library brought specialized areas of expertise to the planning of the workshop. Academic Computing Services (ACS) provided hardware and software expertise, and the library provided content and searching expertise. After the initial planning stage, librarians worked on creating handouts for the sessions as specialists from the computer center worked on preparing the computer lab for instruction.

One of the basic components of a successful collaborative effort was exemplified in this case by the very clear-cut *goal* that was identified by the faculty survey and then in discussion at the initial workshop planning sessions. It was obvious from this survey and subsequent planning discussions that faculty members wanted to have thorough training in the use of the Internet. Both ACS and the library had been providing Internet training. This workshop gave both departments the opportunity to collaborate on reaching a shared goal.

A shared *structure* was set up to meet this goal. More specific data were requested from faculty who expressed a desire for more training. Several solutions were discussed, but finally it was decided to use a workshop format. Specific workshop content was planned. A schedule was created. Each team member had specific tasks, but responsibility for monitoring the implementation of these tasks was shared by the group. One reason for the workshop's success was the team's attention to a shared structure.

Finally, this article identified the *shared benefits* of such a collaborative effort. One of the unplanned benefits mentioned was the general feeling of camaraderie that was generated by this team-conducted workshop. Feelings of goodwill toward the library and ACS were generated. The authors mentioned that additional collaborative ventures in the form of more complex workshops on web page publishing also resulted from this initial effort.

The three-day workshop was viewed as a collaborative success by faculty attendees: "A couple of participants even said it was the best faculty development workshop they had ever attended." Several positive comments concerned the "sense of camaraderie and collegiality" that the group experienced. The authors wrote, "All three of the instructors agreed that neither ACS nor the Library could have offered such an effective workshop on its own."[21]

Types of Connections

Looking at formal collaboration has given us a basis for discussing other types of alliances. According to Himmelman, at least three different types of connections can be formed: networking, coordination, and collaboration.[22] Of the three, networking is the least formal, with collaboration being the most structured. As was discussed in the previous section, collaboration has a formal and relatively complex structure.

Networking

Himmelman described networking as "exchanging information for mutual benefit."[23] A librarian who creates connections by attending a workshop sponsored by a campus professional development committee on teaching students to think critically could be said to be networking. Classroom faculty of like concern would be at this meeting as well. Librarians interested in critical thinking could share and receive ideas from faculty classroom colleagues interested in the same subject. The potential exists to use this networking experience as a basis for a more formal type of connection.

Coordination

Coordination is more formal than networking. Whereas connections made via networking usually include only the exchange of information, coordination builds on networking. Coordination usually implies that two parties will actually work toward a solution to a common problem. An example of this might be the librarian who has attended the campus workshop on teaching students to think critically. She or he might create a one-hour presentation on the subject as applied to undergraduate library research. The librarian might then contact one of the classroom faculty members who attended the same workshop to arrange to give the presentation for a class. The classroom faculty member may have already given an assignment that works toward the goal of teaching students to think critically, as well. Both these colleagues are working toward the same goal, to help students think critically, but each is working independently to a degree. Whereas networking entails sharing information about a common goal, coordination implies that each party has begun an action independently to move toward that goal.

Collaboration

Collaboration invokes a more complicated method of creating connections. Collaboration, as previously defined, is a more structured relationship that is created to solve a common problem. Collaboration goes beyond coordination by adding a structure that ensures a desired alliance actually meets its goal. If the librarian and the classroom faculty member decided to work together to create a series of assignments for a course to teach critical thinking skills, this could be viewed as collaboration. Coordination involves working individually toward a common goal, whereas collaboration involves a more formalized structure. The librarian and the classroom faculty member could meet together, plan the assignment, work out a joint presentation schedule, work on presentation scripts, give the presentation, have the students complete a related assignment, and evaluate the results.

An Example of the Types of Connections: A Comprehensive Liaison Program

In an article titled "Liaison Program + Information Technology = Getting Your Foot in the Door," Beth L. Mark and Soo K. Lee, librarians at Messiah College, described a concerted effort to ensure that faculty members' library needs were being adequately met.[24] The librarians at Messiah created a "comprehensive liaison program incorporating almost all library functions, including selection, weeding and preservation, budget-building and interpretation, non-routine reference assistance, bibliographic instruction, online searching, and cataloging consultation."[25] Each librarian was assigned several academic departments and became an "advocate" and "troubleshooter" for them.

This library reorganization includes examples of all three types of connections discussed earlier. After some internal organization and planning, these librarians began a public relations *networking* campaign. They sent letters to faculty describing new technology and "offering individual and/or group demonstrations."[26] They continued to network with faculty by keeping open communication with informal phone calls, notes, and the like. Difficult assignments observed at the reference desk also initiated opportunities for discussion.

Mark and Lee also described their efforts at *coordination*, particularly through library instruction. By beginning with faculty who were already incorporating library assignments, liaison librarians coordinated with these colleagues by providing short instruction sessions.

These efforts at making connections paid off for the librarians at Messiah by resulting in several more complex *collaborative* efforts. Mark and Lee wrote "This past year both of us participated with faculty in our liaison departments in presenting workshops."[27] They also described a successful collaborative effort in "applying for a teaching grant."[28]

Mark and Lee, after admitting that this effort resulted in a lot of extra work, remarked that "the information needs of both faculty and students are most successfully met through an active liaison program."[29] Networking, coordination, and collaboration represent different ways that librarians can reach out to others in the campus community. A comprehensive liaison program is but one example of how this can be accomplished. No matter the complexity of the relationship, it is important for librarians to create connections with the campus community. Part three of this essay provides more specific examples of networking, coordination, and collaboration.

PART THREE: EXAMPLES OF LIBRARIANS WHO HAVE CREATED CONNECTIONS

The number of articles in the library literature that describe examples of librarians making connections with the rest of the academic community is overwhelming. As worthy and enlightening as each of these articles is, it would be impossible in a setting such as this to discuss each one. Instead, exemplary articles representing each of the three types of creating connections—networking, coordination, and collaboration—are summarized.

Networking

As has been suggested, networking is an important type of connection that primarily consists of the exchange of mutually beneficial information. The first article in this section to be highlighted describes a faculty luncheon established to present important information about the library. The second article is a twist on this same format. Instead of inviting colleagues into the library to give them information, this article describes a program where colleagues were invited into the library to present information to the librarians about their respective schools. The third article describes the extensive networking efforts of a collection development librarian. Each of these articles provides valuable insight into ways that connections can be created via networking.

Luncheon and Information Exchange

In their article "Library Luncheon and Update: Teaching Faculty about New Technology," Julie Banks, Linda Carder, and Carl Pracht, librarians at Southeast Missouri State University, described a successful buffet luncheon and information-sharing session organized by the library.[30] This effort started as an attempt to introduce new faculty members to the library at the ubiquitous new faculty orientation. Along with "free" food, the new faculty were provided with a "glimpse of available services as well as the opportunity to meet library personnel."[31] The number of lasting contacts the librarians made at these luncheons caused them to think about expanding the effort to all campus faculty. The program was amplified by "inviting each college in turn during the academic year to a luncheon, followed by an update of library services and offerings, especially electronic reference and the Internet."[32]

The authors felt that these sessions were a very worthwhile way to network with faculty. They reported that the luncheons brought about an increase in requests for course-integrated library instruction sessions from faculty who attended. Their ultimate measure of success occurred when a college dean called and asked to be invited because of the "positive feedback from across campus."[33] As a result of the contact with colleagues made via these luncheons, the role of the Kent Library as the "key campus information agency" was strengthened.[34]

Inviting Colleagues to Speak to Library Staff

In an article titled "Building Bridges Across an Academic Community," Ursula Mulder, collection management librarian at Curtin University of Technology in Australia, wrote about a program called "Building Bridges" sponsored by the liaison librarians to gather much-needed information to enhance collection development efforts.[35] Nine heads of schools were invited to address the library staff regarding their specific schools. Over the course of a year, these individuals came to the library at various scheduled times to give a short talk about their programs, their academic plans for the next five years, and their research and library needs.

These sessions provided library staff with a wealth of information on campus programs. In these short talks, the library staff heard about new program initiatives. A secondary benefit of the sessions was that library staff were finally able to put faces to names. Typically, networking efforts such as this occur by having librarians talk to faculty, but in this case the reverse had equally positive benefits.

Collection Development
In her article "Liaison with Teaching Faculty: Effective Strategies for Collaborative Collection Development," Christine Wondolowski Gerstein, collection development librarian at Hofstra University, delineated a number of outreach strategies that she uses to ensure that collection building is a collaborative venture.[36] She organized the discussion of her strategies into three areas: liaison activities, public relations activities, and general campus involvement. Her primary bit of advice for emphasizing her role as a departmental liaison was to attend faculty department meetings. This provides scheduled time outside the library where information can be exchanged. She takes every public relations opportunity possible to "bring the library to the attention of the teaching faculty."[37] For example, she routinely sends a letter of introduction to the chairpersons of her assigned departments. Campus involvement is the third area in which she suggested connections can be made. One good idea she shares is to enroll in a course in one of the assigned areas of responsibility. Enrolling in a course not only demonstrates interest in the department, but it also provides the librarian with the opportunity to become aware of the "academic level of both students and faculty."[38]

These proactive networking efforts will help to strengthen the bond, that needs to exist between the liaison librarian and teaching faculty. This relationship can help toward building a balanced library collection.

Coordination
Coordination is an effort on the part of two or more individuals to work toward a shared goal. It implies that each person in the relationship is working toward the end goal in a relatively independent fashion. The first article in this section describes a very typical, but extremely valuable, way that librarians often use

to forge connections—library instruction. The second article is a bit more unusual in that an English department faculty member is invited to step into the world of the library to provide a term paper clinic. Both articles are examples of exciting ways to create connections.

Bibliographic Instruction

In an article titled "Faculty Liaison: A Cooperative Venture in Bibliographic Instruction," Charlotte Cohen, reference/ bibliographic instruction librarian at the American Graduate School of International Management, depicted an effort at coordination between the instructor of "an experimental advanced course dealing with management information systems" and two librarians.[39] These three academic colleagues met to discuss the need for introducing students to information sources they would encounter in actual job situations. They decided to meet this need by offering an instructional session during the course that would introduce students to successful search strategies on two relevant databases. This initial cooperative venture led quickly to library instruction sessions in three more of the faculty members' courses.

Cohen wrote that she gained valuable experience in "targeted program planning" and pointed out that "a carefully outlined proposal when presented to a receptive faculty member could lead to a mutually satisfying cooperative venture."[40]

A Term Paper Clinic

In an article titled "Using English Department Library Liaisons in a Term Paper Clinic," Peter G. Christensen, lecturer in the department of English, describes an interesting coordination between the library and the English department at Marquette University.[41] Typically, when one thinks of a term paper clinic, one thinks of a librarian holding a structured (or sometimes unstructured) session where students can get help with their research. But in this case the faculty member set up shop in the library. "This liaison project grew out of frustration with the often-noted limitations of early-semester library instruction."[42] Several

English department faculty "spent ten hours per week in the library consultation room, available to help students in 65 sections of English 001...with their term paper assignments."[43] In essence, this was a type of specialized reference desk function incorporated into the other activities of the main reference area. Faculty were invited into the realm of the library.

Christensen reported that students who made use of this service greatly appreciated it. Better term papers also were a result. He stated, "we found that students who used the service throughout the semester improved their writing."[44] Much of the success of this program, he felt, could be attributed to the fact that this consultation actually took place in the library "where liaisons could take the students directly to the materials, and read and analyze them together with the students."[45]

Collaboration

Collaboration is the most complex type of connection discussed in this essay. Unlike coordination, collaboration always needs some type of a structure in order to be successful. Members of a collaborative effort work in a teamlike setting toward a common goal. The two articles in this section describe concerted and complex efforts to create connections. The first article describes a librarian and a classroom faculty member who team teach a course. The second article describes a joint effort by a computer trainer and a librarian to present a series of Internet workshops. Although collaboration involves much more work than networking and coordination, the long-term benefits of this type of alliance make the effort well worth the time spent.

Team Teaching

In their article titled "Instruction in Developing Grant Proposals: A Librarian-Faculty Partnership," Paul G. Kussrow and Helen Laurence of Florida Atlantic University wrote about team teaching a course entitled "Grantsmanship and Proposal Development."[46] A librarian team teaching a course with a faculty colleague is probably one of the most privileged forms of collaboration conceivable on an academic campus. A major segment of the audience for their course comprised professionals who "have advanced degrees but little or no formal training in grantsmanship or the use of modern library resources."[47] Kussrow, who is professor of educational leadership, has as a primary course goal to increase the odds of funding of the proposals developed by the students. Laurence, who is associate university librarian, reference department, has two goals for the course: (1) to introduce students to the basic electronic research process, and (2) to introduce students to the specific sources in the field of sponsored research and grant writing.

This team of academic professionals has judged this effort to be a collaborative success. Students of the course reported that as a result of this instruction, their ability to prepare and submit grant proposals increased significantly. At the time this article was written, students had submitted seventy-three proposals to funding agencies. As the authors said, "Teaching this course is rewarding for both instructor and librarian."[48]

Providing Internet Instruction
In their article, "Internexus: A Partnership for Internet Instruction," Sally Kalin, a member of the computer-based resources and services team, and Carol Wright, a basic skills specialist, both at the Pennsylvania State University's Patee Library, described a collaboration to teach Internet skills to the campus community.[49] A campus planning team was created to address the problem of the need for Internet training at Penn State. It was decided to offer a series of workshops presented collaboratively by members of the library and members of Computer and Information Services. Each constituency brought unique strengths and resources to the team. The resulting training program, called Internexus, had as a primary objective to create proficient users of the Internet who could discover "applications in their own fields."[50]

This effort proved so successful that it was presented at several Penn State branch campuses, as well. This collaborative program advertised the library's expertise in technological efforts and garnered much goodwill across the Penn State campuses.

CONCLUSION

The current academic climate has created a ripe opportunity for librarians to become a vital part of the instruction of college students. Librarians have become the campus experts at accessing electronic information. They can connect with the campus community in a number of different ways. It is possible for librarians to forge complex relationships with their classroom faculty colleagues in the realm of networking, coordination, and collaboration.

Librarians are currently creating countless connections with the other components of the campus community. Networking efforts such as luncheons and information exchanges are being undertaken. Coordination efforts, primarily in the realm of library instruction, are being inaugurated. And, as described here, complex collaborative relationships in the form of team teaching and workshop design are being shaped.

It seems that libraries are indeed taking their proactive role quite seriously. The library is truly becoming the "heart of the campus."

NOTES

1. J. Young, "Faculty Collaboration and Academic Librarians," *Catholic Library World* 66 (1995): 17.

2. A.G. Lipow, "Outreach to Faculty: Why and How," in *Working with Faculty in the New Electronic Library: Papers and Sessions Presented at the 19th National LOEX Library Instruction Conference Held at Eastern Michigan University, May 10–11, 1991*, ed. Linda Shirato (Ann Arbor, Mich.: Pierian Pr., 1992): 8; L. Mullins, "Partnerships in Information Teaching and Learning: Building a Collaborative Culture in the University Community," *New Jersey Libraries* 26, no. 1 (1993): 19.

3. Young, "Faculty Collaboration and Academic Librarians," 18.

4. B. Baker, "Bibliographic Instruction: Building the Librarian/Faculty Partnership," *Reference Librarian* 24 (1989): 312.

5. G. Fernandez, "Librarians and Teachers in Partnership," *Florida Libraries* 39 (Jan./Feb. 1996): 9.

6. C. J. Stoffle, A. E. Guskin, and J. A. Boisse, "Teaching, Research, and Service: The Academic Library's Role," in *Increasing the Teaching*

Role of Academic Libraries, ed. T. G. Kirk (San Francisco: Jossey-Bass, 1984), 3–14.

7. Ibid., 5.

8. Ibid., 3

9. Fernandez, "Librarians and Teachers in Partnership," 9.

10. P. W. Mattessich and B. R. Monsey, *Collaboration: What Makes It Work* (St. Paul, Minn.: Amherst H. Wilder Foundation, 1992), 7.

11. D. G. Appley and A. E. Winder, "An Evolving Definition of Collaboration and Some Implications for the World of Work," *Journal of Applied Behavioral Science* 13, no. 3 (1977): 279–91.

12. A. T. Himmelman, "On the Theory and Practice of Transformational Collaboration: From Social Service to Social Justice," in *Creating Collaborative Advantage,* ed. C. Huxham (London: Sage, 1996), 19–43.

13. Mattessich and Monsey, *Collaboration,* 28.

14. Appley and Winder, "An Evolving Definition of Collaboration and Some Implications for the World of Work," 279–91.

15. Mattessich and Monsey, *Collaboration,* 7.

16. Ibid., 24.

17. Himmelman, "On the Theory and Practice of Transformational Collaboration," 19–43.

18. C. Huxham, "Collaboration and Collaborative Advantage," in *Creating Collaborative Advantage,* ed. C. Huxham (London: Sage, 1996), 1–18.

19. Mattessich and Monsey, *Collaboration,* 7.

20. Jane T. Bradford, Kelly E. Kannon, and Susan M. Ryan, "Designing and Implementing a Faculty Internet Workshop: A Collaborative Effort of Academic Computing Services and the University Library," *Research Strategies* 14 (fall 1996): 234–45.

21. Ibid., 243.

22. Himmelman, "On the Theory and Practice of Transformational Collaboration."

23. Ibid., 27.

24. Beth L. Mark and Soo K. Lee, "Liaison Program + Information Technology =Getting Your Foot in the Door," in *Working with Faculty in the New Electronic Library: Papers and Sessions Presented at the 19th National LOEX Library Instruction Conference Held at Eastern Michigan Uni-*

versity, May 10–11, 1991, ed. Linda Shirato (Ann Arbor, Mich., Pierian Pr., 1992): 107–19.

25. Ibid., 107.

26. Ibid., 107.

27. Ibid., 109.

28. Ibid., 109.

29. Ibid., 110.

30. Julie Banks, Linda Carder, and Carl Pracht, "Library Luncheon and Update: Teaching Faculty about New Technology," *Journal of Academic Librarianship* 22 (Mar. 1996): 128–30.

31. Ibid., 128.

32. Ibid.

33. Ibid., 129.

34. Ibid.

35. Ursula Mulder, "Building Bridges across an Academic Community," *Australian Academic & Research Libraries* 23 (Dec. 1992): 175–78.

36. Christine W. Gerstein, "Liaison with Teaching Faculty: Effective Strategies for Collaborative Collection Development," *Public & Access Services Quarterly* 1, no. 4 (1995): 85–90.

37. Ibid., 88.

38. Ibid., 89.

39. Charlotte Cohen, "Faculty Liaison: A Cooperative Venture in Bibliographic Instruction," *Reference Librarian* 51/52 (1995): 161–69.

40. Ibid., 168.

41. Peter G. Christensen, "Using English Department Library Liaisons in a Term Paper Clinic: Reviving the Scholar/Librarian Model," *Research Strategies* 12 (fall 1994): 196–208.

42. Ibid., 197.

43. Ibid.

44. Ibid., 200.

45. Ibid.

46. Paul G. Kussrow and Helen Laurence, "Instruction in Developing Grant Proposals: A Librarian–Faculty Partnership," *Research Strategies* 11 (winter 1993): 47–51.

47. Ibid., 47.

48. Ibid., 51.

49.   Sally Kalin and Carol Wright, "Internexus: A Partnership for Internet Instruction," *Reference Librarian* 41/42 (1994): 197–209.

50.   Ibid., 201.

Case Studies in Collaboration: Lessons from Five Exemplary Programs

Introduction

Scott Walter
Ohio State University

In 1989, the *Chronicle of Higher Education* reported on the proceedings of a conference on "teaching and technology" held near the Richmond, Indiana, campus of Earlham College. Earlham had hosted regular conferences dedicated to fostering instructional collaboration between academic librarians and members of the classroom faculty since the late 1970s, but this conference has been remembered frequently in the literature because of the concerns participants raised about recent advances in information technology that threatened "to leave students adrift in a sea of information."[1] Earlham College librarian Evan I. Farber and his fellow speakers called on conference attendees to develop new teaching strategies that would help students learn how to evaluate and make use of the "masses of information" now accessible to them through emergent information technologies, and to embrace a collaborative teaching model that would allow academic librarians and classroom faculty members to work together in developing instructional objectives appropriate to the information age.[2]

39

As Doug Cook shows in his essay for this collection, academic librarians have taken the lessons of that conference to heart over the past decade. Reports of collaborative approaches to information literacy instruction have become so numerous in recent years, in fact, that any attempt to fully enumerate them is impossible in an essay of this length. Thus, as in Cook's essay, this essay highlights a limited number of exemplary cases of collaboration between academic librarians and classroom faculty members as a means of suggesting broad categories of collaborative activity within which the reader might position his or her own work. Inevitably, not all the institutions that might provide valuable case studies in collaboration are included. However, the case studies that are included should provide the reader with a range of valuable examples and a framework within which he or she may consider future studies.

Among the institutions selected for examination in this essay are familiar ones such as Earlham College, which has long been synonymous with the "course-integrated" model of information literacy instruction, as well as programs of more recent vintage. The "instructional teams" model found at Indiana University-Purdue University at Indianapolis, for example, demonstrates how interest among academic librarians in collaborative approaches to information literacy instruction can support other recent instructional initiatives on campus, such as first-year-experience programs. Likewise, the UWIRED program at the University of Washington has demonstrated how campuswide interest in the educational applications of information technology may be leveraged by academic librarians into extensive opportunities for collaborative instruction. Finally, initiatives such as the College Librarian program at the Virginia Polytechnic Institute and State University and the Faculty Rotation program at the Evergreen State College provide models for fostering collaboration between librarians and faculty members in both the classroom and the institutional administration.

Each of the programs selected for study in this essay demonstrates the fact that interest among the academic library community in collaborative approaches to instruction and in promoting information literacy skills across the entire university community comes at a good time. As P. S. Breivik, Breivik and E. Gee, and H. Rader have shown, the rise in professional interest in information literacy issues among librarians in the past decade is closely related to more general concerns within the educational community, especially the desire to foster critical thinking skills among the student body.[3-5] Professional organizations such as the National Education Association, accrediting bodies such as the Middle States Association of Colleges and Schools, and even state legislatures now incorporate information literacy competencies into proposals for educational reform, for both the public schools and institutions of higher education.[6]

The confluence over the past decade of new priorities in educational reform with rapid developments in information technology provided a perfect opportunity for academic librarians to develop and implement formal information literacy programs on their campuses, and to assume a higher profile in terms of classroom instruction. Even though some of the programs selected for study in this chapter predate this recent surge in interest among the educational community in information literacy, each demonstrates how effective experiments in instructional collaboration between librarians and classroom faculty can meet the educational objectives of both the library and the parent institution.

*** * ***

Earlham College
Collaboration through Course-Integrated Instruction

Jennie Ver Steeg
Northern Illinois University

If nothing else, the Earlham College bibliographic instruction program has generated a formidable paper trail. The program has been featured in library literature for thirty years, even, as former director Evan Farber points out, before the phrase "bibliographic instruction" was in wide use.[7] Of course, much more can be said of the program and of the remarkable Earlham Zeitgeist of collegiality and care.

Modern bibliographic instruction dates from the mid-1960s, when Earlham's program began, and the program has been considered the exemplar or benchmark almost since its modest beginnings. Begun in 1965, "in self defense," the program came to national prominence at the 1969 ALA conference, when Farber's presentation on course-integrated library instruction drew a surprising 800 attendees.[8] Many forces worked to shape Earlham's course-integrated instruction program in its early years. The educational reforms of the 1960s, consonant with Earlham's own institutional values, may have been part of the "secret of its success." Also, whether as a result of the philosophical shifts in higher education or as a part of the whole fabric of social change, there was an "intense preoccupation" with library instruction in the late 1960s and early 1970s.[9] From 1977–1992, first Earlham, then Earlham and Eckerd Colleges, sponsored conferences that focused on the collaboration of teaching faculty and librarians in providing library instruction, partly to stem the pilgrimage of individual librarians coming to see the Earlham College program firsthand.[10]

Identifying the reasons behind the success of the Earlham program, however, proves frustrating. The program is so ingrained in the life of the college that it has been called a way of life.[11] Ninety-four percent of 1993 graduating seniors had had six or more library instruction sessions in their undergraduate careers.[12] It is an academic "of course," so much a part of campus culture, that asking why it is so is rather like asking why we have academic freedom—or rest rooms.

A college of 1,100 students, half of them from the Midwest, and 108 faculty members, the numbers paint a lovely picture: one lab computer per ten students, eleven students to one faculty member.[13, 14] On paper, it is the archetypal Midwestern college of Hollywood movies. The library's statistics paint a more modern picture. The 375,000 monograph volumes and 1,200 print journals in Lilly Library and Wildman Science Library are supplemented by access to 7,200 sources through e-journals and aggregate databases. A member of three consortia, PALNI (Private Academic Library Network of Indiana), the Oberlin Group, and INCOLSA, Earlham has access to Firstsearch, DIALOG, and Lexis-Nexis resources. Its consortial catalog provides access to 13 million volumes.[15] The library employs 6.2 FTE staff, including 2.4 reference/instruction librarians, and a science librarian, a position rare for a small institution.

According to a 1997 study, the average Earlham graduate has library instruction built into 37 percent of all courses taken, though some departments involve the library as collaborator more often than others do.[16] Ninety percent of all political science courses, for example, involve some kind of course-integrated library assignment/ instruction, as do 82 percent of history courses. In the 1997–1998 academic year, 73 percent of full-time teaching faculty utilized course-integrated library instruction.[17] Seventy to eighty percent of Earlham faculty incorporate bibliographic instruction into at least one course taught; indeed, the curriculum "demand[s] library use."[18]

Put simply, Earlham doesn't "do" much one-shot instruction. Instruction occurs in response to an assignment developed in collaboration between a teaching faculty member and a librarian, and the librarian typically meets with a class, as a class or in small work groups, several times during the course of an assignment. Assignments are constructed to ensure early successes, then build on skills attained during the course of an assignment (sometimes assigned twice in a course or twice in a sequence of discipline courses). The approach is described as sequenced, structured, and progressive; or more poetically, course-related, demonstrated, and gradated.[19] It tends to result in highly structured assignments, with a topic determined by the instructor and the librarian (the librarian "presearches" the assignment to ensure the student can succeed using resources available). The assignment includes clear expectations regarding length, format, number, and types of sources used. The end product—whether a poster presentation, pathfinder, Web page, or term paper—is usually due in a short time period to work against procrastination.[20–22]

Each Earlham student is assured of some library instruction, first with the library skills test as a part of freshman orientation. Then as part of the general education–required courses humanities A and B, students meet the librarian, have some experience with resources, and receive a list of resources specific to the course and topic of the assignment. Initially, the focus is on students' getting a sense of the library as an important place at Earlham and of the librarian as a valuable colleague in the course of their education. In students' major courses, course-related instruction is likely to present itself in innovative assignments; many of Earlham's assignments have been written about in library literature.[23] Evan Farber noted that the ideal library assignment is one in which faculty member and librarian aims are complimentary and, at the very least, a good assignment makes reading a term paper less boring.[24]

An example of a course-integrated assignment is the "Responsible Patient" assignment, used in both introductory biology classes and in an upper-level anatomy class. This activity requires students to use first, popular, and then, primary, secondary, and other resources to evaluate the safety and effectiveness of commonly prescribed treatments for common conditions, such as asthma. The student is given two opportunities to complete the assignment in the course of a semester, with the goal of understanding the nature, organization, and means of access to scientific literature. Another goal, however, is student empowerment; the student may have to do such research in his or her lifetime.[25] Earlham's science library and course-integrated instruction in the sciences are all the more impressive, given a study cited by S. Penhale which uncovered that out of ninety-six undergraduate institutions, only five to ten percent of students receive instruction in how to use scientific literature.[26]

Bibliographic instruction, however, is only the most visible evidence, one result of a unique culture of collaboration. Director Thomas Kirk wrote that course-integrated instruction is a part of a "systematic dialogue between librarian and faculty member," resulting not only in instruction, but also in the construction of better assignments and better use of the collection by students and faculty.[27-29] That faculty would welcome this type of collaboration says a great deal about the Earlham ethos.

Founded in 1847 as a boarding school for Quaker children, in 1859, it became the second Quaker College in the world.[30] Although the majority of faculty and students are not now Friends; the college is still affiliated with the Friends, and its community code, relatively flat administrative structure, governance by faculty consensus, and campus involvement in issues of social justice and peaceful resolution of conflict still reflect an unusual campus culture. Although it is not unusual for a college to emphasize teaching and learning, the Earlham campuswide value of collaboration is unique. The Earlham College mission statement reads:

> The teaching–learning process at Earlham is shaped by a view of education as a process of awakening the "teacher within" . . . The College provides extensive opportunities for students and faculty to interact with each other as persons . . . an important aspect of which is collaborative student/faculty research.[31]

Earlham's small size and emphasis on dialogue and consensus makes the development of collaborative relationships between teaching faculty and librarians, as well as between faculty and students, a natural state of affairs. This is reflected by the other ways in which the library seeks dialogue with teaching faculty. Librarians are included in interviews of job candidates, meeting and giving a tour to each; the library director speaks at new faculty orientation (as well as at freshman orientation) and sends a letter of welcome to each new faculty member—and actually follows up with a meeting. Also, an individual librarian functions as instructional, reference, and faculty liaison librarian, so that each faculty member develops relationships with an individual librarian in a variety of contexts: as support for faculty teaching and research, as a collection development source, as a source of professional information, as troubleshooter, and, ultimately, one hopes, as coequal colleague.[32]

Thus, it would not be much of a stretch to characterize Earlham's program of library instruction to be a tangible result of the value of relationships as a part of the Earlham campus climate. Even the goals of instruction reflect this value; although it is true that students are expected to learn information-seeking and evaluation skills, other goals mentioned in the literature include helping students to overcome anxiety, empowering students to be better consumers of health information, and reinforcing collaborative relationships with faculty and librarians as partners in a student's education.[33, 34]

The campus value placed on collaboration (and, by extension, on relationships) is enmeshed so thoroughly in campus climate that it seems mystical, cabalistic—what can one take from Earlham's experience? Luckily, this value is expressed in some fairly straightforward and surprising ways. Because it is everybody's right to accept or reject the value of libraries and library instruction, it does little good to try to promote bibliographic instruction to disinterested faculty.[35, 36] Kirk adds that he believes it takes at least ten years to develop a library instruction program.[37] The role of time, word of mouth, and incremental change are seen as the most important ways a program can grow and become a viable part of the college—starting small and growing slowly. Rather than thinking of ways to promote the library, it might be more productive to think of ways to promote learning at the institution, for, as Farber wrote, "the library is not the heart of the institution, the teaching–learning process is."[38] At Earlham, bibliographic instruction is not seen as a service and is not marketed as such; it is not, in fact, marketed at all. Advisors, colleagues, memos, orientations, faculty meetings, college publicity materials—all tend to mention and publicize the library already, as part of the teaching–learning process. More marketing, one supposes, would be overkill, like advertising the benefits of breathing—both in and out.

Instead, the library and course-integrated instruction are promoted through the power of relationships. G. Thompson, a professor of English literature at Earlham, stated that the success of bibliographic instruction is dependent on a process of "seduction," with the first steps taken by the librarian, adding that a shared interest is the best foundation for all collaboration in teaching. He also recommended that librarians become involved in campus committees, team teaching, grant writing, or college governance to make the connections with the faculty, which would make them powerful, noting that, "librarians with power are in a much better position to make bibliographic instruction programs succeed . . . . The long-term goal should be the creation of a critical mass of B.I. advocates."[39] With a mature instruction program, the library needs to maintain and reinvigorate itself continuously, continually training new faculty and new students and inculcating the value of libraries to the Earlham campus. It is particularly important to keep offering course-integrated instruction on the use and evaluation of electronic resources.

At Earlham, the library has been a leader in the adoption of technology on campus, an example of which was the introduction of DIALOG to campus in the early 1990s. The library received funding to sponsor a campus-wide forum to discuss issues surrounding technology and its implications for classroom teaching and student learning. Dissatisfied with faculty response, the library received a Lilly grant and contacted DIALOG, proposing to act as a kind of pilot project for unmediated campus access to DIALOG databases. DIALOG, interested in gathering information about the academic market, agreed to make DIALOG available free for a year campuswide.

The library hired an outside consultant and taught fifteen faculty members to use DIALOG, then had a faculty retreat, at which those faculty members taught other faculty to use DIALOG. During the study, faculty kept logs of their experiences; the library offered assistance and met regularly with faculty groups. Of course, many important findings were serendipitous and unexpected, but in the end, faculty and students did have a better understanding of one particular technology, their research methods had changed, and, most important, collaboration between faculty and students increased.[40]

For all that the library instruction program has, Earlham's program notably lacks many of the elements the *ALA/ACRL Guidelines for Instruction Programs in Academic Libraries* recommends: the program has no statement of purpose, projected outcomes, detailed plan, timetables, goals, plan of evaluation, and budget.[41] Farber wrote that the definition and measurement of success are by no means set, each library constituency may define success differently, and given the emphasis on the teaching–learning process, the success of the library instruction program cannot be measured separately from the success of the library as a whole.[42] There have been small, targeted assessments of the reach of the program and of students' attitudes toward the library and their own searching skills, using focus groups, surveys of alumni, and anecdotal evidence, such as the perceptions of students returning from internships.

In 1997, Earlham College librarians conducted a larger and more ambitious evaluation of the program's reach, using graduates' transcripts, the course catalog and bibliographic instruction records to determine which departments made the most use of instruction sessions and what the average student might experience in a given department. The results showed a wide range of departmental involvement with the library and an overall picture of the average student receiving course-integrated instruction in 37 percent of all his or her classes.[43]

Though Earlham's structure and philosophy may make it unique, one difference is thought-provoking for instructional librarians in any type of institution. The Earlham library instruction program does not have its own budget line, nor does it offer a separate information skills or information literacy course. More important, no one is disturbed by the lack of either. As Kirk noted, "The program is so thoroughly integrated ... and so central to the mission and the goals of the institution that it has never been isolated budgetarily."[44] A separate line item is vulnerable to being cut in response to budget crunches or shifts in campus politics. For the same reason, Farber pointed out the inadvisability of offering a separate information skills course. Although the students in such a class may be given interesting assignments, the assignments are still not integrated with the students' other courses; at worst, they are context-free busy work. The idea that information-seeking skills are integral to all the students' studies is not being reinforced. Also, if such a course is part of a general education requirement, many students who are not interested in the topic will only have their disinterest further nurtured with busy work assignments. Conversely, if it is an elective, librarians would likely be preaching to the choir, attracting students already convinced of the worth of information skills. Finally, and most compelling, a separate course is politically vulnerable. It is easy to cut a course to save money or in response to curriculum change, but one cannot cut an endeavor that is integrated into nearly every course offered. As part of the fabric of all disciplines, and integrated into whatever courses exist, bibliographic instruction is at once ubiquitous and politically invisible.[45]

The Earlham College course-integrated library instruction program, which began as a response to the dreaded problem assignment (a literature professor gave his students tasks difficult even for the reference librarians), has changed its methods somewhat in response to new technologies and changes in the college environment. But as Farber noted in 1995, "plus ça change [the more things change]," the more they stay the same. Faculty still are territorial and tend to teach as they have been taught. Students, despite sophistication and ease with the Internet and other information technologies, still have difficulty discriminating among resources. Earlham's goal, aside from that of collaboration, in the end might boil down to this: "If there were just one skill . . . it should be: Ask the reference librarian."[46]

Earlham College library director Thomas Kirk hesitates to call Earlham's program unique. He characterizes the campus as a close community, with informal social interactions and a high level of service orientation. He notes that "Some long-time faculty will say Earlham today is a 'museum for the best of the social climate of the 1960s,'" but feels the program's beginning had more to do with a fortunate dovetailing of the values of the 1960s with the values already manifested at Earlham.[47] The college's small size and liberal arts tradition may be part of the success of the library instruction program, as well. The function of a library at a baccalaureate institution is to support the curricula, and successful use of a smaller collection virtually demands collaboration between librarian and faculty member just to ensure that the assignment can be accomplished successfully.[48]

Whatever social forces and accidents of history contributed to Earlham's success, the program is singular, one of a kind. Thompson says that "It is probably unwise to copy Earlham practices,"[49] calling it an eccentric institution. Kirk feels such a success may be difficult for larger institutions. Large research universities are less likely to have a similar program, based on "universally held beliefs and character." On the other hand, regarding a humane tradition of education, Kirk observes that "Each generation must re-invent the way that this tradition is expressed."[50] Whether any institution can copy the Earlham College experience is likely beside the point; its innovative role in assignment construction and emphasis on the power of relationships make it a worthy ideal.

✳ ✳ ✳

Indiana University-Purdue University at Indianapolis
Collaboration through Instructional Teams in a First-Year Experience

Sarah Beasley
Portland State University

Indiana University-Purdue University at Indianapolis (IUPUI) is a post–World War II, urban university. Founded in 1969 as a consolidation of the Indianapolis-based professional programs of Indiana University and Purdue University and several other professional schools, IUPUI has grown to become Indiana's third-largest university, serving 27,000 students (three-quarters of whom are undergraduate and 48 percent of whom attend part-time). IUPUI offers the widest array of degree offerings of any campus in the state system and houses its only medical and dental schools, as well as its urban law school. However, because the state of Indiana has only recently begun to provide support for a community college system, IUPUI also has functioned as the regional campus for lower-level undergraduate education, offering open enrollment for central Indiana residents.

Due to its urban setting and program mix, IUPUI has a larger percentage of returning, part-time, older-than-average, low-income, first-generation, and minority students than other campuses in the Indiana system that serve more "traditional" students. These student groups can present a different set of needs and easily flounder in traditional, diversified university campus settings. About IUPUI's undergraduates, Scott Evenbeck, dean of IUPUI's University College, has stated: "Their high school experiences have taught them to enter a post-secondary experience so that they can earn credits, as opposed to gaining knowledge, and thus become qualified for better jobs in business and industry. These characteristics in conjunction with other academic weaknesses can prevent student success at the undergraduate level."[51]

At IUPUI, questions about how to meet the needs of these groups of students began to be addressed through various efforts to boost their success and improve retention. Within the colleges of liberal arts and sciences, various programs emerged to meet these needs. Drawing on principles established in the United States Department of Education's Involvement in Learning report, the Undergraduate Education Center, a centralized advising unit, launched an initiative to establish first-year-experience courses delivered by teams composed of faculty members and various academic support professionals.[52] In 1996, the efforts of the Undergraduate Education Center, with its array of first-year-experience courses and broad charge in supporting undergraduate education, became the University College.

In the fall of 1995, coincident with the evolution of University College and the learning communities model developing there,

Philip Tompkins began his tenure as the IUPUI library director. Tompkins was one of the leaders of the Coalition for Networked Information's (CNI) New Learning Communities (NLC) program. The NLC program brought together participants in innovative instructional programs through a series of conferences in the mid-1990s. Programs participating in the NLC conferences had the following characteristics: "team involvement at every stage; imaginative use of networking resources; focus on students as participants and as active learners; demonstration of incorporation of new information literacy; direct relationship of networked information components of the curriculum; approach worthy of replicability; new approaches to teaching and learning."[53]

Tompkins brought to IUPUI a perspective on learning communities, team organization and the value of multisector instructional teams. The IUPUI library was reorganized into a team structure. This allowed shifting within the library so that more librarians could serve on a newly developed library instruction team. In the fall of 1996, members of the library instruction team began working as members on the University College Instructional Teams.

The IUPUI Instructional Teams model braids together three models prevalent in higher education: learning communities, first-year-experience programs, and multidisciplinary teams. Administratively, the IUPUI Instructional Teams program rests within University College. The college offers a one-credit college experience course that is linked with an introductory required course in the major. A departmental faculty member serves on a team with a librarian, a student advisor, a student mentor, and a computer technologist. The course is developed and delivered from syllabus to final exam by the instructional team. The librarian's involvement typically includes both the collaborative activities of course planning and assessment and the conduct of three to four "interventions" per semester.

In the IUPUI model, the concepts of learning communities and instructional teams marry very nicely. Generally, learning communities can be thought of as:

a variety of curricular models that purposefully restructure the curriculum to link together courses or coursework during the same quarter or semester so that a group of students finds greater coherence in what they are studying and experiences increased intellectual interacting with faculty members and other students. In learning communities, students and faculty members experience courses and disciplines as complementary and connected enterprises.[54]

Coupled with a concern for greater student–faculty interaction and greater coherence in the curriculum, an instructional team approach provides more depth to course work as a broader spectrum of expertise is brought to the table in planning and implementing instruction. In addition to the specific strengths that each team member brings to the program, the team formation and course design processes are in and of themselves extremely important. IUPUI has a specific outline for the phases of team development described in its "Collaborating with Librarians on Instructional Teams" document.[55] What emerges from the team process is "gradual development of a mutual understanding of the group initiative."[56] A paramount benefit of the instructional team process is that learning objectives that previously may have been thought of as the province of one department or one team member become a part of the syllabus for the course and are shared by the entire instructional team. In regard to library instruction, this goal is furthered by the presence of librarians on the curriculum committee of University College.

In the fall of 1996, five IUPUI librarians participated on instructional teams for twenty-three courses. By the following year, there were forty-six courses; by fall 1998 seventy-eight sections were served by nine librarians, and by fall 1999 one hundred and thirty sections will be served by sixteen librarians. The program's growth is a mark of its success but clearly presents problems in terms of meeting increased demand for courses that utilize the instructional teams model. In addition to serving on instructional teams, the IUPUI instruction team librarians maintain work assignments on other library teams.

William Orme, IUPUI library instruction team leader, sees the Instructional Teams model as part of a future in which information literacy and research instruction are part of an articulated curriculum throughout undergraduate education at IUPUI. He also notes that complete adherence to the Instructional Teams model has not been embraced in all the courses: some departmental faculty are suspicious of University College and have tolerance, but not necessarily enthusiasm, for the Instructional Teams model. Orme notes, though, that roughly one quarter of the teams are functioning as the model outlines. He states: "You take your successes where you find them." He places IUPUI's efforts firmly in the tradition of the Earlham course-integrated instruction model but feels that IUPUI librarians enjoy the benefit of earlier intervention. Their interaction is at the point where the syllabus is "still up for grabs," and the librarians' involvement with the faculty occurs when "the course outline, the resources to be used for teaching and learning, teaching methods, assignments and assessment measures" are still being developed.[57]

IUPUI University College assessment efforts have included tracking the retention levels and grade-point averages for first-year students (both of which have gone up). Orme states that "Clearly, students are gaining academically." The IUPUI library has undertaken pre- and posttesting of students in the Instructional Teams classes, and although a preliminary look at the data showed an increase in students' research abilities, the library is awaiting further data analysis from the university's research office.

The Evergreen State College
Collaboration through Faculty Rotation

Scott Walter
Ohio State University

As is the case at IUPUI, instructional collaboration between librarians and faculty members at The Evergreen State College (Olympia, Washington) reflects deeper currents of reform in American higher education. Whereas IUPUI benefited from administrative interest in the recent trend toward the development of "learning communities," instructional collaboration at Evergreen is rooted in a long-standing institutional commitment to the educational reform initiatives typical of the "experimental" colleges and universities of the 1960s. As with Earlham College, the commitment to instructional collaboration at Evergreen is an expression of an organizational culture that values interdisciplinary education and collaborative decision making, in both the classroom and the administration. As one faculty member wrote after a decade of experience, Evergreen "is committed to collaborative teaching as its primary mission."[58]

In their landmark study of educational change in higher education, *The Perpetual Dream: Reform and Experiment in the American College*, Gerald Grant and David Riesman described the era of the 1960s as being "as volatile a period of educational reform as America has ever experienced."[59] Chartered in 1967, and accepting its first students for admission in 1971, Evergreen was one of several experimental colleges and universities of the era that attempted to address popular concerns about the quality of undergraduate education by embracing a new approach to teaching and learning on the college campus.[60] Sharing with other experimental schools a common set of commitments to interdisciplinary, student-centered education, and egalitarianism in decision making, Evergreen abandoned familiar administrative structures such as faculty tenure and organization by academic department and embraced a distinctive approach to classroom teaching referred to as the "coordinated studies program."[61-63]

The coordinated studies program is an interdisciplinary, team-based instructional model that allows a group of faculty and students to study a single topic for an extended period of time. Bearing titles such as "Human Development," "The Individual in America," "The Sixties," and "Power in Perspective," these programs typically engage eighty to a hundred students and four to five faculty members, full-time, for an entire quarter (or even an entire year). During the school's first year (1971–1972), over 90 percent of the student body was enrolled in a coordinated studies program; during the fall 1998 quarter, student participation remained at over 70 percent.[64, 65] Whereas other educational options have developed in order to allow for greater flexibility in scheduling (e.g., independent study), the interdisciplinary coordinated studies program remains the hallmark of the instructional program at Evergreen.[66]

For faculty members, the institutional commitment to the coordinated studies program requires a personal commitment to instructional collaboration. As noted above, coordinated studies programs are conducted by an instructional team, and this team is responsible for the development, delivery, and assessment of its program from start to finish. Given the broad scope of these programs, team members are typically required to teach and to lead seminar discussions in areas of study outside their own specialties. Faculty members are regarded as "co-learners," but also as "expert learners, capable of transferring from their own specific fields 'generic' problem-solving expertise for acquiring and weighing information pursuant to investigating research problems."[67] In other words, faculty members are recognized as being information literate and as having the ability to transfer their abilities to teach (and to learn) in their own fields to the corollary fields also being addressed in their coordinated studies programs. As Sarah Pedersen has noted, this is an instructional model highly conducive to participation by academic librarians.[68]

When the first faculty appointment of a librarian was made in 1977, Evergreen's classroom faculty were charged with finding a way to integrate librarians into their collaborative approach to curriculum development and classroom teaching. Since 1978, faculty librarians at Evergreen have had the opportunity to participate in a "rotation" program with classroom faculty that brings librarians into the classroom and members of the classroom faculty into the library. The rotation program, described by one participant as being "unique in American academic librarianship," requires librarians to rotate onto a faculty team for one quarter out of every nine (but allows for greater flexibility as required, sometimes allowing a librarian to teach full-time for two consecutive quarters in order to remain part of an ongoing program).[69, 70] During the rotation, librarians are released from their normal duties and assume the responsibilities of a member of the classroom faculty for the collaborative guidance of a coordinated studies program.[71]

T. Hubbard has noted that participation in the rotation program allows librarians to bring their instructional skills into "the mainstream of the curriculum," to further develop personal contacts with the classroom faculty, to more closely observe faculty methods of teaching, to gain a greater insight into faculty research interests, and to participate in the academic counseling and guidance of students outside the library setting.[72] Other veterans of the rotation program also have concluded that participation by librarians in this program can have a positive effect on their professional development as teachers and as researchers and can help to bring new approaches to classroom teaching into the realm of traditional information literacy instruction.[73, 74]

Participation by librarians in the rotation program also reinforces their position as members of the teaching faculty. As F. Hill and R. Hauptman have noted, the issue of faculty status for academic librarians revolves around the question of the degree to which librarians fulfill professional responsibilities similar to those of classroom faculty members.[75] The faculty rotation program at Evergreen provides a model in which those responsibilities are identical. M. Huston and F. Motley reported that the rotation program "insured our recognition as full-fledged members of the faculty."[76] Pedersen concurred, saying that "We have significant influence in governance and in service to our academic community and that influence extends far beyond our role as representatives of the library; we function fully as teachers in the administrative work of the college."[77] As evidence of their place in the faculty community, Evergreen librarians have served as members of all-campus committees, as coordinators of academic programs, and even as academic deans.[78]

Participation in faculty rotation also supports the librarian's teaching role outside the coordinated studies program. Evergreen librarians teach in rotation, but they also participate in all other instructional options available to Evergreen students, including individual learning contracts (i.e., independent study), group learning contracts, and traditional information literacy instruction.[79] Evergreen librarian Frank Motley, for example, reported that he has supervised "dozens" of individual learning contracts in addition to his regular rotation into coordinated studies programs such as "Mark Twain" and "Techniques in Social Science Research."[80] Huston and Motley reported that librarian participation in the rotation program raises student awareness of "the academic qualifications and abilities of librarians," and that this is clearly reflected in the continuing role librarians have in supervising student learning in programs other than the ones into which they have rotated.[81]

Traditional information literacy instruction also has benefited from librarian participation in the rotation program. In 1981, Huston and Motley reported that student comments suggested that exposure to a librarian as a member of an instructional team in a coordinated studies program had a positive effect on the likelihood that the student would later enroll in the library's for-credit research course.[82] Four years later, Huston and Parson reported that the research course itself had been reshaped in response to librarian participation in the rotation program.[83] Information literacy instruction at Evergreen became increasingly collaborative in conduct as faculty librarians brought the collaborative approach to instruction that they observed in the coordinated studies program back to the library.[84] Today, although Evergreen no longer offers a regular, stand-alone research course, library faculty continue to offer occasional information literacy "programs" that reflect their experience with teaching in rotation.[85] As Pedersen et al. concluded: "The most intriguing aspect of the library is the teaching, which is a direct or indirect function of an unusually high percentage of the staff members who successfully apply the tenets of the Evergreen teaching philosophy in their instruction."[86]

Faculty and student participation in course-related instruction also has been positively influenced by librarian participation in the rotation program. Pedersen echoed a familiar sentiment among Evergreen librarians when she wrote that "the rotation strongly enhances the likelihood that our faculty colleagues will seriously consider our contribution to their teaching in the form of bibliographic instruction."[87] In 1996–1997, for example, eighty-nine course-related instructional sessions reached 4,877 students. In 1997–1998, the same number of programs reached 4,814 students. Although these numbers include some "double counting" (students whose coordinated studies programs included more than one instructional session) as well as instructional sessions conducted as an outreach activity to local high schools, it is clear that, as Dean of Library Services William Bruner has concluded: "we get deeply into the curriculum each year."[88] Instructional collaboration within the context of the rotation program, then, promotes a high level of instructional collaboration within the more familiar context of course-related information literacy instruction.

The Evergreen State College is a relatively small school. Enrollment stands at approximately 4,000 students, and its Daniel J. Evans Library holds just over 250,000 volumes. This collection is maintained by a staff of thirty-six professionals, three staff librarians (nonfaculty), one media faculty member (nonlibrarian), and six faculty librarians. Despite its small size, Evergreen's long experiment with interdisciplinary education and instructional collaboration has had a significant effect on the rhetoric of educational reform at the postsecondary level. In a report on institutional collaboration between Evergreen and Seattle Central Community College, for example, Smith and Hunter noted the rising interest among the educational community in collaborative approaches to teaching and learning in higher education, and linked the instructional model provided by the coordinated studies program to the current work represented by "learning communities."[89] As we have already seen in the case of IUPUI, administrative support for learning communities can become an important bridge to instructional collaboration between librarians and classroom faculty members. In its way, then, Evergreen has served as a "lighthouse" school, showing the way for others who have come to embrace the idea of full-fledged instructional collaboration within the community of classroom faculty members, and between classroom faculty members, and academic librarians.

Burton R. Clark has written on the ways in which a distinctive organizational culture can have a powerful effect on the practice of teaching and learning in institutions of higher education.[90] It follows, therefore, as Pedersen et al. have written, that the distinctive character of The Evergreen State College would have an effect on its library, "a key component of organizational culture on campus."[91] At Evergreen, an institutional commitment to interdisciplinary education and collaborative teaching has become embodied in a unique rotation program for classroom faculty members and librarians that offers the latter an unparalleled opportunity to bring their skills and interests into the educational mainstream of the college and to collaborate fully with members of the former in the instruction and guidance of the student body.

✳ ✳ ✳

The University of Washington
Collaboration through Instruction Technology

Mike Tillman
California State University Fresno

The University of Washington (UW) is a research university with an enrollment of more than 34,000 students. Located in Seattle, near Microsoft corporate headquarters, the campus is generally considered to be one of the most technologically advanced universities in the country. Internal reports and presidential proclamations have emphasized the importance of instructional technology and information literacy. The campus and its libraries have benefited from their relationship with Microsoft cofounders Paul Allen and Bill Gates. Allen's father was employed by the UW libraries and a major endowment in his honor has allowed the libraries to participate in innovative initiatives such as UWIRED. Mary Gates Hall, named in honor of Bill Gates's mother, will open in 2000. It will facilitate technology-infused undergraduate education.

The main libraries and twenty-one branches contain almost 6 million volumes. There are 117 librarians and 208 staff members. The libraries value outreach and collaboration. In fact, the libraries have set aside funding for collaborative projects that must include participants from inside and outside the libraries.[92]

Like most academic libraries, UW libraries seek to integrate information literacy into the university curriculum. Unlike some academic libraries, they place great value on technology that facilitates information literacy. According to M. Donovan and A. Zald, "information literacy and information must be seen as intimately connected with the technology that is used to find, retrieve, sort, and otherwise manipulate it."[93] They believe that "understanding the technology that allows us access to information is a foundational skill for citizens of the information age."[94]

The UW libraries also believe in utilizing technology as a tool to further instructional collaboration with faculty members. Due to technological advancement, "faculty are experiencing the need for new technology and information-handling skills" and "are beginning to restructure their courses and teaching methods to utilize networking capabilities."[95] The UW libraries have decided to take full advantage of present-day realities through minor undertakings such as offering workshops on how to develop Web pages. More important, they have entered into major undertakings such as the UWIRED program.

UWIRED, which began in 1994, is an outcome of an initiative put into motion by former UW Provost Wayne Clough. It attempts to bring technology into the service of teaching and learning through the creation of a networked electronic community that emphasizes communication, collaboration, and information technologies as important parts of teaching and learning.[96] Initially, computing and communications, undergraduate education, and the UW libraries came together under the UWIRED umbrella.

During summer 1994, all faculty and staff (including librarians) who were involved with the program received five days of training that covered the Internet, e-mail, software, library resources, etc. Three "freshmen interest groups" (FIGs) were selected to participate in the UWIRED program. FIGs are groups of students who share a particular interest, such as biology or psychology. During autumn 1994, targeted FIGS and their instructors received $4,300 laptops, free of charge. Targeted FIGs also received extended training covering technology and information literacy, and had exclusive access to a "collaboratory" that was built in the undergraduate library adjacent to UWIRED librarians. The collaboratory commingled aspects of a collaboration-friendly classroom and a computer laboratory.

During autumn 1995, the anthropology FIG and the men's and women's basketball teams received laptops and joined UWIRED. Seven additional FIGs also joined UWIRED. The seven additional groups did not receive laptops but did receive extended training and exclusive use of a second collaboratory built in the undergraduate library. Funding was provided for the development of innovative, upper-division courses that incorporated technology. During autumn 1996, all sixty FIGs were brought into the UWIRED fold. None of these students received laptops, but all of them received extensive training and access to three collaboratories located in the undergraduate library. During 1997, information and technology–linked courses were created to tie credit-bearing information literacy training to specific general studies course work.

Since its inception, UWIRED has placed a major emphasis on faculty and librarian development. The Teaching and Technology Lecture Series has included lectures such as "Language, Learning, Teaching, and Technology"; "Going Online in Economic Geography: Challenges and Opportunities"; and "Intellectual Property in a Digital Age." UWIRED also established the Center for Teaching, Learning, and Technology, which is located in the undergraduate library next to one of the collaboratories. The center provides consultation services for faculty, teaching assistants, and librarians. Topics covered include information literacy, technology,

and instructional design. An exhaustive UWIRED Web site (http:/
/www.washington.edu/uwired/) provides faculty and staff with
tutorials covering a wide variety of technology-related topics. The
site also showcases innovative courses inspired by UWIRED
funding and/or philosophy.

The UW Office of Education Assessment is involved with
the evaluation of UWIRED. They have employed pre- and
posttesting, polling, surveys, focus groups, and instructor
evaluations. Initial evaluation was formative and focused on
educational processes. Later evaluation sought to measure
educational products. Overall, the program received high ratings
from students and faculty. Collaboration and portability of laptops
were noted as particular strengths of the program. Students believed
that UWIRED participation led to improved performances in all
of their classes. Faculty found that, as a group, UWIRED students
outperformed other students. Students significantly increased their
ability to browse the Internet, exchange e-mail, and join electronic
discussion groups.[97]

UWIRED was awarded the 1995 Association of College and
Research Libraries, Bibliographic Instruction Section's Innovation in
Bibliographic Instruction Award. It continues to bring technology
into the service of teaching and learning. Through participation in
UWIRED, the UW libraries are attempting to integrate information
literacy into the curriculum. The program brought structure and
recognition to an extensive instruction program that had always been
happening but had not been given a name.[98]

Through the years, UWIRED instructional technology has
fostered significant, sustained collaboration between faculty and
librarians. From the beginning, UWIRED technology brought
faculty and librarians together. They received technology training
together and then developed course work that integrated the
technology. Laptops and collaboratories caught the attention of
the campus, state legislature, and the bibliographic instruction
universe. L. Wilson noted that UWIRED has developed a "halo
effect" and others from across campus seek to become involved
with the program.[99] Faculty interest in the program and its related

technologies provided librarians with an opportunity to help faculty master the latest technologies. The incorporation of instructional technology into linked and innovative courses brought librarians and faculty together during the formative stages of instruction. Innovative courses also provided librarians with opportunities to serve as on-site technical and content resources providing assistance on an as-needed basis.[100]

Collaboratories; the Center for Teaching, Learning, and Technology (CTLT); the UWIRED Teaching and Technology Lecture Series; and the UWIRED Web site are less obvious examples of technology-related UWIRED features that have fostered collaboration. The collaboratories and CTLT are located in the library and bring faculty into the library to teach and learn. CTLT consultants (including librarians) provide faculty assistance with course-related technology. The UWIRED Teaching and Technology Lecture Series attracts large numbers of faculty and librarians, and provides librarians with an opportunity to showcase their knowledge. The UWIRED Web site disseminates examples of collaboration between librarians and faculty.

Future library-related UWIRED initiatives will help sustain the program. They include engaging entire academic departments in the development of discipline-specific information literacy.[101] Moreover, plans are under way to offer instruction covering the knowledge structure of various disciplines. J. Scepanski has asserted that future libraries "will be viewed as a program rather than any particular place."[102] If his vision of the future comes to pass, the UW libraries will have been well served by their participation in UWIRED.

✳ ✳ ✳

The Virginia Polytechnic Institute and State University
Collaboration through Faculty Outreach

Susan Ariew
Virginia Polytechnic Institute and State University

In a recent article in *College & Research Libraries,* "Improving Library Relations with the Faculty and University Administrators: The Role of the Faculty Outreach Librarian," S. Stebelman et al. pointed to studies indicating that librarians are generally viewed more as subordinates than as equals to the teaching faculty. The authors offered several suggestions to raise the status of academic librarians within the academic community. One approach is embodied in the outreach librarian position at George Washington University, held by a librarian with a Ph.D. as well as a library degree.[103]

The outreach librarian is described as someone who implements proactive outreach activities with faculty by setting up services such as electronic lists, e-mail communications, faculty brown-bag luncheons, and timely newsletters. Outreach activities tend to cluster around the use of electronic resources. Indeed, Stebelman et al. suggested that academic librarians, in general, should align themselves with computer technology and electronic resources in attempting to define their instructional role. They wrote that librarians will "be more successful if they teach electronic resources more than conventional ones, which faculty believe they already have mastered."[104]

Putting the emphasis on technology as the key to higher status for librarians seems somewhat misplaced, however, given the fact that faculty and administrators will eventually master that new frontier themselves (thus eliminating the need for librarians as technology gurus). Moreover, there are always others in the academic community to fill the role of technology expert, and normally they, too, are not people who are identified as "equals" of the academic teaching faculty. Instead of looking to expertise in the use of computer technology and electronic information resources to raise the status of librarians, one should look to the collaborative interpersonal relationships created by the librarian and his or her role in the academic scheme of things. If the librarian is truly collaborating with faculty on meaningful projects related to the faculty's teaching and research, equity and respect for the librarian's skill and expertise will naturally follow, whether they related to computer technology or not.

So how do librarians build strong, equitable, proactive relationships with faculty and administrators such that opportunities for collaboration flourish? In an attempt to answer this question, Virginia Polytechnic Institute and State University (Virginia Tech) created the College Librarian Program. Virginia Tech is the state's largest university. It serves almost 26,000 students (on and off campus), 80 percent of whom are undergraduates. Aside from the student population, the library supports the research and teaching of approximately 1,500 full-time instructional faculty. From the beginning, Virginia Tech has offered highly centralized library services. Even today, despite the fact that Virginia Tech has four branch libraries (Art and Architecture, Geosciences, Veterinary Medicine, and the Northern Virginia Graduate Center), most of its collection is housed and maintained in Newman Library. The collection consists of more than 1.9 million printed volumes, 17,000 serial subscriptions, 5 million microforms, 130,000 audiovisual and machine-readable pieces, and 120,000 maps. The library is staffed by approximately thirty-five tenure-track faculty and one hundred forty staff members. Before the College Librarian Program was initiated, the university libraries promoted the traditional roles for librarians as both subject specialist bibliographers and reference experts, and provided services from a library-centered model.

In an attempt to shift to a more user-centered service model, the College Librarian Program began as a pilot program in 1994 with four librarians serving the Colleges of Education, Human Resources, Agriculture, and Arts and Sciences. Unlike the George Washington model discussed above, in which the outreach librarian rarely gets out of the library and into the work environment of faculty and administrators, each of these college librarians was housed in the college, rather than in the library.[105] The library director and the vice president for information systems planned and supported this program both administratively and financially. These administrators met with the deans of all the colleges to create a unique program that emphasized outreach and service to users in their own work environments. Through the efforts of both library and college administrators, each college librarian was given an office in his or her college, equipped with state-of-the art computers, printers, and a small collection of ready-reference material.

At first, librarians in these offices did work similar to that of traditional librarians: responding to reference questions, consulting with faculty and students on their research projects, and planning and coordinating library instruction activities. Although the work was what one would call "traditional," the collaborative process was improved by the increased opportunity for contact with students and faculty members. This was especially the case in the area of instruction.

For example, the college librarian for human resources worked with faculty in the hospitality and tourism department to integrate library instruction into the curriculum for all new majors in the field. In collaboration with department faculty, he developed online instructional tutorials customized to the basic research needs for the introductory class in hospitality and tourism. Later, his successors developed a library instruction component for Human Resources 1104, the basic class all students entering the college must take. By collaborating with faculty who taught the required introductory course for the college, the college librarian for human resources assured that students would be exposed to basic library instruction for networked and print resources in their fields. Collaborative instructional efforts such as these reflect a true partnership between librarians and faculty attempting to integrate curriculum with information literacy skills in a holistic way. These kinds of ongoing instructional efforts by all the college librarians would not be possible without first building strong relationships with the faculty.

With the rise of the Internet as an instructional resource and the increasing use of technology by students and faculty, librarians made use of newly purchased library-networked resources to create "virtual branches" in their colleges. The college librarians blended these new services into their work with their constituencies, which provided opportunities for collaboration as well. For example, as college librarians notified faculty and students about added networked services such as the WinSPIRS databases, they were called upon to help them with installing the library client software in their offices and to teach them how to use the new services. Each semester, the library has added new networked services, and one of the many ways it publicizes them is through the day-to-day contacts college librarians have with their clients in their work environments.

When some faculty struggled with developing Web pages, using Internet resources in their classes, or creating online courses and programs, librarians became colleagues who were valuable sources of expertise. Librarians were valued not because they were HTML experts or technology gurus but, rather, because they could discuss the application of technology to instructional purposes and provide a link to the library infrastructure that supports Web-based instruction.

For example, in responding to the need to deal with the information explosion presented by the Internet during 1994–1997, the college librarians created their own subject-specialty Web pages.[106] These pages met the need to identify relevant databases available through the library network, as well as other resources (reference materials, directories, etc.) that could be delivered to their faculty and students electronically. Thus, librarians were able to form strong relations with faculty not only because of their technology skills, but also because working with faculty closely on a day-to-day basis allowed librarians to respond more readily to their needs.

Most important, allowing library/information services to take place in the college environment meant that relationships could grow on a more informal basis. Being housed in their respective colleges offered college librarians the opportunity to become part of the life of the college. Rather than just attending the occasional faculty meeting, for example, librarians were invited to serve on college and departmental committees and task forces, to apply for grants with faculty, and to work with faculty on linking library resources to online courses for distance education projects. At present, the college librarian for agriculture is a member of the dean's staff and also serves on the college coordinating academic advisor's council for the College of Agriculture. As part of a group of administrative leaders, she is aware of developments in her college and offers library-related support where it is relevant.

Likewise, the college librarian for education and human development has served as a member of several departmental committees over the years. As a member of the standards of learning committee and the diversity committee, she has offered information resources and support for committee projects. Both committees awarded grant monies for purchase of instructional software materials and videos for the college librarian's office, which is located in the teaching and learning department. With the creation of a new online master's program in health and physical education, the college librarian for education was invited to participate in the planning stages and throughout the program, making sure that extended campus users could connect and use networked resources in the program from a distance. Clearly, many of these activities went beyond "outreach" and into real collaborative efforts because of the day-to-day nature of the work being done with faculty.

Given the growth of closer and more meaningful relationships with faculty and librarians through this program, one could see an increase in the demand for the services of librarians in colleges, that did not have a college librarian. For example, in 1995, the Business and the Engineering Colleges requested the services of college librarians; and librarians in those disciplines were added to the program. In 1996-1997, at the request of the dean of Arts and Sciences, the largest of the colleges at Virginia Tech, two more librarians were assigned to the College Librarian Program in Arts and Sciences, so that the program now includes a humanities, science, and social sciences college librarian. The pilot program that began in 1994 with four librarians has grown to include ten college librarians.

Outreach statistics also show a growth in demand for library instruction for the university libraries because of the College Librarian Program. In 1995–1996, the four college librarians taught 3,559 students in 170 instructional sessions. The eight librarians in 1996–1997 taught 5,829 students in 273 sessions, with over 60 percent more students and class sessions from the previous year. Instruction statistics continue to rise each year. To keep up with the increase in demand, the library has added more resources to the instruction program: additional electronic classrooms equipped with state-of-the-art computers, broadcasting equipment for the electronic classrooms, new software, instructional equipment that can be taken out to classrooms in the colleges, and teaching assistants to help with the added demand for library instruction.

The success of the program is reflected in the growth in instruction statistics and in two surveys conducted with faculty. College librarians conducted a preliminary survey in 1996, and then another one in the spring of 1998 distributed by e-mail to faculty. Survey methodologies and results are discussed in the article, "Outreach through the College Librarian Program at Virginia Tech."[107] Clearly, any institution that wishes to initiate a program such as the College Librarian Program should be prepared for growth—and a budget to support that growth because successful outreach and collaborative efforts create a demand for more services.

Of course, without administrative support, the program could not have thrived as it has. Initially, the College Librarian Program was instituted and overseen by the vice president for information systems and the director of the university libraries. The librarians were seen as being on the front line in terms of providing Internet/technology support. However, since that time, the library reporting system has changed. This indicates a shift in how the program is perceived on campus. The deans of libraries and library personnel now report directly to the provost, who asserted: "This switch will more closely link the library function with the academic enterprise of the university." The provost goes on to point out that "This change recognizes the close and continuing ties of library goals with the university's academic mission, the opportunities for joint projects in support of research and teaching that exist between colleges and the library, and the essentially academic nature of the core of library operations." The vice president for information systems supported this move, asserting that "This change in reporting relationship will continue the effort initiated several years ago, though the College Librarians Program, to integrate library resources with the rapidly changing needs of the colleges."[108] This administrative decision alone illustrates the fact that librarians and academic faculty are seen as partners and, indeed, peers in their research and teaching efforts. It has been fueled by close collaborative efforts and recognition of those efforts within each college.

The College Librarian Program has filled a need at Virginia Tech and will continue to be the means by which the university libraries keep in touch with their patrons. Like traditional branch librarians, college librarians can provide customized service, instruction, and information resources at the users' location. Unlike traditional branch libraries, the costs of staffing and maintaining a specialized, physical library collection are lacking. Hence, one sees a new, efficient, centralized library model that allows for the "high-touch" elements of personal assistance and the development of relationships with faculty. These in turn provide productive, collaborative opportunities that result in more equitable relationships between academic librarians and teaching faculty.

NOTES

1. T. DeLoughry, "Professors Are Urged to Devise Strategies to Help Students Deal with 'Information Explosion' Spurred by Technology," *Chronicle of Higher Education* 35 (Mar. 8, 1989): A13, A15.

2. Ibid.

3. P. S. Breivik, *Student Learning in the Information Age* (Phoenix, Ariz.: Oryx Pr., 1998).

4. P. S. Breivik and E. Gee, *Information Literacy: Revolution in the Library* (New York: Macmillan, 1989).

5. H. Rader, "Information Literacy and the Undergraduate Curriculum," *Library Trends* 44, no. 2 (1995): 270–78.

6. Breivik, *Student Learning in the Information Age*, 7–8; K. Spitzer, with M. Eisenberg and C. Lowe, *Information Literacy: Essential Skills for*

the Information Age (Syracuse, N.Y.: ERIC Clearinghouse on Information and Technology, 1998), 50–58.

7. E. Farber, "Plus Ça Change," *Library Trends* 44, no. 2 (1995): 430–38.

8. J. Kennedy, T. Kirk, and G. Weaver, "Course-Related Library Instruction: A Case Study of the English and Biology Departments at Earlham College," *Drexel Library Quarterly* 7, no. 3–4 (1971): 277–98.

9. Ibid.

10. L. Hardesty, "Preface," in *Bibliographic Instruction in Practice: A Tribute to the Legacy of Evan Ira Farber: Based on the 5th Earlham College–Eckerd College Bibliographic Instruction Conference February 5–7, 1992*, ed. Larry Hardesty, Jamie Hastreiter, and David Henderson (Ann Arbor, Mich.: Pierian Pr., 1993), v–vi.

11. S. Taylor, "Successful Bibliographic Instruction Programs at Three Small Liberal Arts Colleges," *Research Strategies* 11, no. 4 (1993): 242–47.

12. S. Penhale, N. Taylor, and T. Kirk, "A Method of Measuring the Reach of a Bibliographic Instruction Program," 1997 [cited 24 July 1999]. Available from <http://www.ala.org/acrl/paperhtm/d29.html>.

13. Thomas Kirk, electronic communication to Jennie Ver Steeg, 25 July 1999.

14. Earlham College, "Earlham College…at a Glance," n.d. [cited 24 July 1999]. Available from <http://www.earlham.edu/at_a_glance.html>.

15. Thomas Kirk, electronic comunication to Jennie Ver Steeg, 23 Feb. 1999.

16. Penhale, Taylor, and Kirk, "A Method of Measuring the Reach of a Bibliographic Instruction Program."

17. Kirk, electronic comunication, 23 Feb. 1999.

18. Taylor, "Successful Bibliographic Instruction Programs at Three Small Liberal Arts Colleges."

19. Kennedy, Kirk, and Weaver, "Course-Related Library Instruction."

20. E. Farber and S. Penhale, "Using Poster Sessions in Introductory Science Courses: An Example at Earlham," *Research Strategies* 13, no. 1 (1995): 55–59.

21. F. Rasmus and C. Larson, "Instructional Partnerships: Team Teaching Global Politics and the Web," *Indiana Libraries* 16, no. 1 (1997): 43–48.

22. S. Penhale, "The Role of Bibliographic Instruction in the Improvement of Undergraduate Science Education," in *Bibliographic Instruction in Practice: A Tribute to the Legacy of Evan Ira Farber: Based on the 5th Earlham College – Eckerd College Bibliographic Instruction Conference February 5–7, 1992,* ed. Larry Hardesty, Jamie Hastreiter, and David Henderson (Ann Arbor, Mich.: Pierian Pr., 1993), 63–66; S. Penhale, J. Woolpy, and W. Buskirk, "Learning to Be a Responsible Patient," *Research Strategies* 9, no. 1 (1991): 51–55.

23. E. Farber, "Bibliographic Instruction at Earlham College," in *Bibliographic Instruction in Practice: A Tribute to the Legacy of Evan Ira Farber: Based on the 5th Earlham College – Eckerd College Bibliographic Instruction Conference February 5–7, 1992,* ed. Larry Hardesty, Jamie Hastreiter, and David Henderson (Ann Arbor, Mich.: Pierian Pr., 1993), 1–25; Farber and Penhale, "Using Poster Sessions in Introductory Science Courses"; B. Hall, "Bibliographic Instruction in the Social Sciences," in *Bibliographic Instruction in Practice*; Penhale, "The Role of Bibliographic Instruction in the Improvement of Undergraduate Science Education"; ———, "Cooperative Learning Using Chemical Literature," *Science and Technology Libraries* 16, nos. 3–4: 69–75; Rasmus and Larson, "Instructional Partnerships"; W. Stephenson, "A Developmental Approach to Bibliographic Instruction," in *Bibliographic Instruction in Practice*, 27–40; G. Thompson, "Sequenced Research Assignments for the Undergraduate," in *Bibliographic Instruction in Practice*, 41–50.

24. Farber, "Bibliographic Instruction at Earlham College."

25. Penhale, Woolpy, and Buskirk, "Learning to Be a Responsible Patient."

26. Penhale, "The Role of Bibliographic Instruction in the Improvement of Undergraduate Science Education."

27. Kirk, electronic comunication, 23 Feb. 1999

28. Evan Farber, "Alternatives to the Term Paper," in *Bibliographic Instruction in Practice: A Tribute to the Legacy of Evan Ira Farber Based on the 5th Earlham College–Eckerd College Bibliographic Instruction Conference February 5–7, 1992,* ed. Larry Hardesty, Jamie Hastreiter, and David Henderson (Ann Arbor, Mich.: Pierian Pr., 1993), 89–96.

29. ———, "Bibliographic Instruction at Earlham College."

30. T. Hamm, "A Brief History of Earlham College," 1998 [cited 24

July 1999]. Available from <http://www.earlham.edu/EC_history.html>.

31. Earlham College, "Earlham College Mission," n.d. [cited 24 July 1999]. Available from http://www.earlham.edu/mission.html (24 July 1999).

32. Farber, "Bibliographic Instruction at Earlham College"; Hall, "Bibliographic Instruction in the Social Sciences"; Thompson, "Sequenced Research Assignments for the Undergraduate".

33. Farber, "Alternatives to the Term Paper."

34. Penhale, Woolpy, and Buskirk, "Learning to Be a Responsible Patient."

35. Kennedy, Kirk, and Weaver, "Course-Related Library Instruction."

36. Hardesty, "Preface."

37. Taylor, "Successful Bibliographic Instruction Programs at Three Small Liberal Arts Colleges."

38. Farber, "Bibliographic Instruction at Earlham College," 1.

39. G. Thompson, "Faculty Recalcitrance about Bibliographic Instruction," in *Bibliographic Instruction in Practice: A Tribute to the Legacy of Evan Ira Farber: Based on the 5th Earlham College – Eckerd College Bibliographic Instruction Conference February 5–7, 1992*, ed. Larry Hardesty, Jamie Hastreiter, and David Henderson (Ann Arbor, Mich.: Pierian Pr., 1993), 104.

40. A. Beth and E. Farber, "Lessons from DIALOG: Technology Impacts Teaching/Learning," *Library Journal* (Sept. 15, 1992): 26–28.

41. Taylor, "Successful Bibliographic Instruction Programs at Three Small Liberal Arts Colleges."

42. Farber, "Bibliographic Instruction at Earlham College."

43. Penhale, Taylor, and Kirk, "A Method of Measuring the Reach of a Bibliographic Instruction Program."

44. Kirk, electronic comunication, 23 Feb. 1999.

45. Farber, "Bibliographic Instruction at Earlham College."

46. Farber, "Plus Ça change," 436.

47. Kirk, electronic communication, 25 July 1999.

48. Penhale, Woolpy, and Buskirk, "Learning to Be a Responsible Patient."

49. Thompson, "Faculty Recalcitrance about Bibliographic Instruction."

50. Kirk, electronic communication, 25 July 1999.

51. S. Evenbeck and M. Foster, "The Urban First Year Experience: Building Community Benefits Faculty and Other University Professionals and Serves Students Well" (paper presented at the Ninth International Conference on the First Year Experience, St. Andrews, Scotland, 1996), 4. ERIC ED 418 608.

52. U. S. Dept. of Education. National Institute of Education (U. S.). Study Group on Conditions of Excellence in American Higher Education, *Involvement in Learning: Realizing the Potential of American Higher Education* (Washington, D.C., 1984), 2.

53. P. Tompkins, S. Perry, and J. Lippincott, "New Learning Communities: Collaboration, Networking, and Information Literacy," *Information Technology and Libraries* 17, no. 2 (1998): 100.

54. B. Smith, "Taking Structure Seriously," *Liberal Education* 77, no. 2 (1991): 42.

55. S. Hay, "Collaborating with Librarians on Instructional Teams," 1998 [cited 14 June 1999]. Available from <http://www.ulib.iupui.edu/itt/ulit.html>.

56. Tompkins, Perry, and Lippincott, "New Learning Communities," 102.

57. Hay, "Collaborating with Librarians on Instructional Teams"; W. Orme, conversation with Sarah Beasley, 8 June 1999.

58. R. Jones, *Experiment at Evergreen* (Cambridge, Mass.: Schenkman, 1981), 33.

59. G. Grant and D. Riesman, *The Perpetual Dream: Reform and Experiment in the American College* (Chicago: Univ. of Chicago Pr., 1978), 1.

60. Jones, *Experiment at Evergreen*; W. Stevens, "The Philosophical and Political Origins of The Evergreen State College," (Ph.D. diss., Univ. of Washington, 1983); B. Youtz, "The Evergreen State College: An Experiment Maturing," in *Against the Current: Reform and Experimentation in Higher Education*, ed. Richard M. Jones and Barbara Leigh Smith (Cambridge, Mass.: Schenkman, 1984), 93–118; J. Rosenzweig, "The Innovative Colleges and Universities of the 1960s and 1970s: What Keeps the Dreams of Experimentation Alive?" (paper presented at the ASHE annual meeting) 1997. ERIC ED 415 810.

61. Rosenzweig, "The Innovative Colleges and Universities of the 1960s and 1970s," 5–6.

62. C. McCann, "Academic Administration without Departments at The Evergreen State College," in *Academic Departments: Problems, Variations, and Alternatives*, ed. Dale E. McHenry et al. (San Francisco: Jossey-Bass, 1977).

63. M. Levensky, "Trying Hard: Interdisciplinary Programs at The Evergreen State College," *Alternative Higher Education* 2, no. 1 (1977): 41–46; Jones, *Experiment at Evergreen*.

64. Youtz, "The Evergreen State College," 98.

65. W. Bruner, electronic communication to Scott Walter 22 July 1999.

66. G. Kuh et al., *Involving Colleges: Successful Approaches to Fostering Student Learning and Development Outside the Classroom* (San Francisco: Jossey-Bass, 1991), 233–37; Bruner, electronic communication, 22 July 1999.

67. M. Huston and W. Parson, "A Model of Librarianship for Combining Learning and Teaching," *Research Strategies* 3, no. 2 (1985): 76.

68. Sarah Pedersen, electronic communication to Scott Walter, 1 June 1999.

69. T. Hubbard, "Teaching in Rotation as a Member of the Instructional Faculty and as a Librarian," in *The Librarian in the University: Essays on Membership in the Academic Community*, ed. H Palmer Hall and Caroline Byrd (Metuchen: Scarecrow Pr., 1990), 109.

70. Bruner, electronic communication, 22 July 1999.

71. M. Huston and F. Motley, "Faculty Membership for Librarians: The Evergreen State College Model," in *Options for the 80s: Proceedings of the Second National Conference of the Association of College and Research Libraries*, vol. 2 (Greenwich, Conn.: JAI Pr., 1981), 413–19; M. Huston, "Research in a Rotation Librarian/Faculty Program," *College & Research Libraries News* 46, no. 1 (1985): 13–15; Hubbard, "Teaching in Rotation as a Member of the Instructional Faculty and as a Librarian."

72. Hubbard, "Teaching in Rotation as a Member of the Instructional Faculty and as a Librarian."

73. Huston, "Research in a Rotation Librarian/Faculty Program."

74. Huston and Parson, "A Model of Librarianship for Combining Learning and Teaching," 78–79.

75. F. Hill and R. Hauptman, "A New Perspective on Faculty Status," *College & Research Libraries* 47, no. 2 (1986): 156–59.

76. Huston and Motley, "Faculty Membership for Librarians," 414.

77. Pedersen, electronic communication, 1 June 1999.

78. Ibid.

79. S. Pedersen, J. Espinola, M. Huston, and F. Motley, "Ethnography of an Alternative College Library," *Library Trends* 39, no. 3 (1991): 339–41.

80. F. Motley, electronic communication to Scott Walter, 9 June 1999.

81. Huston and Motley, "Faculty Membership for Librarians," 417.

82. Ibid.

83. Huston and Parson, "A Model of Librarianship for Combining Learning and Teaching."

84. Ibid., 78–79.

85. Bruner, electronic communication, 22 July 1999.

86. Pedersen, Espinola, Huston, and Motley, "Ethnography of an Alternative College Library," 337.

87. Pedersen, electronic communication, 1 June 1999.

88. Bruner, electronic communication, 22 July 1999.

89. B. Smith and M. Hunter, "Learning Communities: A Paradigm for Educational Revitalization," *Community College Review* 15, no. 4 (1988): 45–51.

90. Burton R. Clark, "Belief and Loyalty in College Organization," *Journal of Higher Education*, 42, no. 6 (1971): 499–520.

91. Pedersen, Espinola, Huston, and Motley, "Ethnography of an Alternative College Library," 336.

92. L. Wilson, "The Way Things Work: Teaching and Learning in Libraries," in *Programs That Work*, ed. Linda Shirato (Ann Arbor, Mich.: Pierian Pr., 1997), 3.

93. M. Donovan and A. Zald, "Defining Moments: The Role of Information Literacy in the 21st Century," 2.

94. Ibid., 10.

95. Rader, "Information Literacy and the Undergraduate Curriculum," 5.

96. A. Bartelstein, L. Fox, P. Steward, L. Wilson, and A. Zald, "UWIRED: Enhancing Teaching, Learning, and Technology through Collaboration," in *LOEX of the West: Collaboration and Instructional Design in a Virtual Environment*, eds. Kari Anderson, Elizabeth Babbitt, Emily Hull, Theresa Mudrock, and Helene Williams (Stamford, Conn.: JAI Pr., 1996), 25.

97. L. Fox and K. Sharpe, "UWIRED: Driver's Ed for the Information Highway," *Educator's Tech Exchange* 3, no. 2 (1995): 20–23.

98. B. Bengston, "Collaborating for the Future," *Library Directions* 5, no. 1 (1994): 1.

99. Wilson, "The Way Things Work," 9.

100. H. Williams and A. Zald, "Redefining Roles: Librarians as Partners in Information Literacy Education" (paper presented at the Second International Symposium on Networked Learner Support, Sheffield, England, 1997), 6. [cited 7 July 1999]. Available from <http://netways.shef.ac.uk/rbase/papers/zald-abs.htm>.

101. L. Wilson, "Information Literacy: Fluency across the Curriculum," (paper presented at the Univ. of Louisville, 1999), 14.

102. J. Scepanski, "Forecasting, Forestalling, Fashioning: The Future of Academic Libraries and Librarians," in *Academic Libraries: Their Rationale and Role in American Higher Education*, ed. Gerard B. McCabe and Ruth J. Person (Westport, Conn.: Greenwood Pr., 1995), 171.

103 S. Stebelman, J. Siggins, D. Nutty, and C. Long, "Improving Library Relations with the Faculty and University Administrators: The Role of Faculty Outreach," *College and Research Libraries* 60, no. 2 (1999): 121–30.

104. Ibid., 122.

105. Ibid.

106. Virginia Tech University Libraries, "Subjects and Liaisons." [cited 22 July 1999]. Available from <http://www.lib.vt.edu/resarch/liaisons.html>.

107. J. Schillie, V. Young, S. Ariew, E. Krupar, and M. Merrill, "Outreach through the College Librarian Program at Virginia Tech," *Reference Librarian* (forthcoming).

108. L. Hincker, "Administrative Reorganization Announced," *Spectrum: News for Staff and Graduate Students* 21, no. 17 (Jan. 21, 1999): 1.

New Science and Collaboration in Higher Education

Dick Raspa
Wayne State University

Dane Ward
Central Michigan University

> "But I don't want to go among mad people," Alice
>   remarked.
> "Oh, you can't help that," said the Cat; "we're all mad
>   here. I'm mad. You're mad."
> "How do you know I'm mad?" said Alice.
> "You must be," said the Cat, "or you wouldn't have
>   come here."
>
> —Lewis Carroll

At the edge of the twenty-first century, we find ourselves in a strange universe, not unlike Alice in Wonderland. Our twentieth-century commonsense world, based on Newtonian mechanics, has shifted to a twenty-first-century quantum cosmology, based on constantly shifting energy patterns. In the quantum universe, many things appear to be non-sense, even maddening, as Alice discovers when she talks to the Cat. What we thought was solid and stable, such as matter, becomes fluid and unstable. Even traditional ways of reasoning from premise to premise to conclusion are turned topsy-turvy. Alice asks for evidence of madness, a request for inductive conventions of proof. Instead, the Cat commits what in traditional logic would be called the fallacy of begging the question: the Cat assumes as true what needs to be proven. He declares Alice's presence as evidence of madness, thereby subverting her request for empirical evidence, evidence of mad or deviant behavior. Ordinary conversation in this universe can feel bizarre, unmoored from familiar categories of logic.

Has our world really been turned upside down? Consider the global shift to a new paradigm that Alvin Toffler calls the "Third Wave" and others refer to as the "information age."[1] According to these social prognosticators, the current transition represents a revolutionary development of the same magnitude as those that transformed humans from hunter-gatherers to farmers and then again from farmers to industrial age denizens. On a personal and organizational level, the rapidity of change frequently leaves us disoriented, reeling in a state of vertigo. In institutions of higher education, the pressure to change the way we work has been driven by new technologies: Web access to a universe of information that expands at exponential rates, proliferating distance education programs, laptops, "ubiquitous computing," courseware, and presentation software, to mention a few.

We frequently become aware of the "madness" of this world when traditional patterns of organizational decision making fail to respond with sufficient speed or knowledge to changing circumstances. Most corporations and institutions operate within a formal framework of relationships that fails to facilitate the flow of information among all those who could offer valuable contributions. Decision-makers are left with few tools and usually resort to organizing task forces and subcommittees to further investigate an issue.

How different our world is today. In the eighteenth century, the world according to Newton was rational, quantifiable, and predictable. We could know it with reasonable certitude and understand how the physical world operated according to laws of gravity and causality. These laws provided human beings with a compass by which to live ordered lives. In the quantum universe of today, predictability and order give way to probability and chaos. To flourish in this emergent world, unfamiliar skills are needed. New science reveals those skills and helps us live in the world differently. According to organizational consultant Margaret Wheatley:

> To live in a quantum world, to weave here and there with ease and grace, we will need to change what we do. We will need to stop describing tasks and instead facilitate *process*. We will need to become savvy about how to build relationships, how to nurture growing, evolving things. All of us will need better skills in listening, communicating, and facilitating groups, because these are the talents that build strong relationships. It is well known that the era of the rugged individual has been replaced by the era of the team player. But this is only the beginning. The quantum world has demolished the concept of the unconnected individual.[2]

The distinguishing feature of the quantum universe is relationship. As Nobel Laureate physical-chemist Ilya Prigogine told us in his research into the relationship between order and chaos, a nonlinear, open system must have a relationship with its environment in order to survive, involving among other factors, for instance, an exchange of energy in the form of food. When a perturbation or disturbance in the environment becomes so great that the system's structure cannot deal with the change, the entity is said to be on the edge of chaos. It is there on the edge that the system can spontaneously leap to a higher order of complexity and integration and, therefore, can evolve spontaneously into a new order. All open systems share this possibility. At the risk of oversimplifying, when human beings are considered as complex, open physical/spiritual systems, we, too, have this opportunity: confronted with a disruption in our lives, we can open ourselves to that force and be renewed and transformed by our relationship with it.

In higher education, we are experiencing a major discontinuity resulting from the continual development and application of new technologies. Some would say *we* are sitting on the edge of chaos. Changing technologies are impacting how we teach, how we research, how we communicate, how we publish. Many of us are actively seeking new strategies for structuring our work in a way that achieves measurable results. Proponents of New Science argue that traditional organization charts will prove ineffective as road maps to this new work environment based on relationships and that we are prepared to jump to a higher level of organization. Perhaps all the talk about thinking and working "out of the box" points to a new way of organizing ourselves, a way of working together that transcends divisions between disciplines and departments.

We live in dynamic systems of energy, swirling in and around us, where everything is related to everything else. Even space is not empty as we may have thought, but filled with invisible structures of energy. The "butterfly effect," discovered by meteorologist Edward Lorenz, notes that a butterfly flapping its wings in Tokyo can affect weather conditions in London. Another quantum insight comes from the Principle of Complementarity that informs us subatomic matter can be either a particle or a wave depending on the expectations of the observer. And Heisenberg's Uncertainty Principle tells us that we can measure an entity's position if we consider matter as a particle and measure movement if we consider it as a wave, but we cannot measure both position and movement at the same time. "In the quantum world," wrote Wheatley, "relationships are not just interesting; to many physicists, they are *all* there is to reality."[3]

Wheatley observed that we are bundles of energy and which energy gets actualized depends on where we are and whom we are with.[4] In other words, which energy is called forth and expressed depends on the degree to which we engage others in relationship. Even the notion of power has been affected by new developments in science. Power is the energy generated by relationships rather than the more static notion of the authority to control or dominate others. The actualization of energies says something about the dynamic, idiosyncratic nature of collaboration. The quality of our working relationships on campus varies considerably. With some people, we are energized by ideas and possibilities; with others, we tend to work in a functional sort of way.

In the new millennium, collaboration will be a process that has been transformed by the new science. In the Newtonian world, we focused on the things of the universe—the materiality of entities that could be empirically validated. In the quantum world, we focus on the stream of relationships that constitute our universe. What difference does this shift make in schools? In educational institutions, hierarchical systems of authority with their beliefs in the rationality of bureaucratic structures, their reliance on the routinization of work, and their goal of predictability of outcomes will shift to fluid organizational structures, with their beliefs in the emergent order inherent in chaotic systems, their reliance on spontaneous forms of work, and their goal of evoking the unfolding of contexts of work. Hierarchical negotiations, as Wheatley said, are replaced by energy exchanges. In the quantum universe, collaboration becomes the dominant mode of working. We will all be collaborators in organizations that can be seen as fields of energy constantly in motion, always changing. The static, solid organization is only one snapshot in time. In the next instant, the organization has moved, provisionally, into another configuration. We live, as physicist David Bohm suggested, like the caterpillar and butterfly— momentary and transient configurations in the flow of the energy.

Does this holistic approach seem improbable? Consider this scenario. In most institutional libraries, we are concerned with quantitative measures of "relevance." We count the number of circulated books, the number of reference questions, the number of library instruction sessions, and take the outcomes as measures of the library's success or failure. In quantum terms, this reflects an odd perspective about the nature of relationships and one that is symptomatic of our tendency to compartmentalize our lives into "places" and "things." Although the library staff may be responsible for "drumming up" business, it is not their "problem" if statistics indicate a decline in use. It is much more dynamic than that, a holistic process that concerns the entire campus, if not the community and society at large. What would it mean if students and faculty used fewer of the services and resources offered by the library? The implications would be profound, suggesting that students are reading, researching, and writing less, reflecting less on their fields of study; and learning fewer of the skills that would permit them to succeed in an information society. Statistics about library use should be topics of discussion all across campus. Instructional faculty should review these statistics in light of their efforts to provide opportunities for meaningful learning. Collaboration is not a question of stepping outside our departments to work together; it is acting from the recognition that we are dynamically and holistically connected in life.

Change is unsettling. Most of us want the feeling of permanence. We want things to hold still long enough for us to understand and, perhaps, even affect them. What is disconcerting about the new work environment—for everyone across industries— is the temporary quality of things. Entities seem to have lost their solid shape, even their solid foundation in unchanging realities. As the Irish poet Yeats said in characterizing the modern world: "Things fall apart; the center cannot hold./Mere anarchy is loosed upon the world."

The contemporary world can fill us with dread. And our work life can be reduced to complaints about how good it used to be and how awful it is now. However, the source of worry can also be the fount of excitement. If we imagine ourselves and others as bundles of energy, potency packs, then when we are with people, energy is activated creating a field of interaction and bringing into being a set of possibilities. Which potentials are summoned depends on how we engage the other. In short, we have more control over what transpires in our lives than we may have thought. We are not hapless victims being swept along by powerful forces outside ourselves. We have a choice about how we will engage the other, and in that engagement, we can bring forth possibilities for new life.

In education, how do we—faculty and librarians—engage each other? Do we see each other as sources of energy? Do we regard colleagues as positive charges that energize our organizational environments and enliven our individual projects? Or do we complain about how working with others drains our energy? Do we dread being in the same office or department or even room with that person or those people, seeking ways to avoid them. When our work life is reduced to complaints, what results is a loss of power to influence events and a shrinking of our presence in the institution. New science helps us to see that we eschew relationships at great cost to our personal effectiveness and success. "There are no recipes or formulae, no checklists or advice that describe 'reality'," wrote Wheatley. "There is only what we create through our engagement with others and with events."[5]

In addition to understanding the power of relationship, new science also helps us to understand how we perceive and organize experience. One instrument that measures the strength of our ways of doing this is the personality preference inventory.

COLLABORATION AND MYERS-BRIGGS

The Myers-Briggs Type Indicator (MBTI) is a scientific instrument for measuring personality preferences. It was developed in the mid-twentieth century by a mother and daughter, Isabel Briggs Myers and Katherine Briggs, who based their inventory on the work of the Swiss psychologist Carl Gustav Jung. The purpose of the MBTI is to increase self-awareness and move toward full expression of the individual. The MBTI can help us understand ourselves and increase our ability to communicate with other people who are different from us.

We are becoming an increasingly diverse workforce in higher education, one in which technologists, librarians, and faculty, with very different life experiences and skills, must work together to meet the challenge of bringing forth powerful student learning. Today, we are encouraged to value differences rather than denying or marginalizing them. As many of us have found, this is a task easier talked about than accomplished. Even with the best of intentions, we often fail to understand each other. Listening under these circumstances produces discomfort and dissatisfaction with results. Effective collaborative relationships depend on a commitment to develop mutual understanding, the willingness to extend our ability to listen to each other. The MBTI is a powerful tool for developing such understanding on campus because it provides us insights into our thought processes and behavior, as well as those of people with whom we might work.

The MBTI permits us to identify personal preferences along four scales: (1) the way we process information, (2) assess it, (3) act on it in the world, and (4) the way we face other people. By referring to preferences, the MBTI makes clear that it does not evaluate the actual ability of individuals to practice each preference. The purpose of the MBTI is to facilitate awareness of our ways of organizing experience and connecting to the world.

The MBTI is not an intelligence test, nor is it a way to classify people, placing them in limiting psychological boxes. Rather, the MBTI reveals that preferences are like folding your hands. Most of us always fold our hands the same way—with the right thumb on top, or the left one. We could fold our hands with either thumb dominant, but we naturally fold into a preferred position. Psychological preferences are like that, too. We have a preferred way of processing or assessing information, though we can also do it the other way, though less adroitly.

Scale 1: Processing Information

The first MBTI scale focuses on our sources of energy and helps us recognize whether we are more "energized" through interactions with others, extraversion, or through periods of quiet reflection, introversion. *Extroversion* and *introversion* are terms that do not carry the evaluative charge that popular culture gives them—that is, that extroverts are perceived as outgoing, vivacious, full of life while introverts are seen as withdrawn, shy, and somewhat depressed. The truth is that the introversion–extroversion distinction is about one thing: the source of energy. Extroverts get it by being with other people; introverts get it by being alone.

Evidence that the popular conceptions of introversion/ extroversion are erroneous is from the world of performance. Many great actors and entertainers—who stand before people and make them laugh or cry by the power of their performance—are introverts, like the comedian Johnny Carson who hosted the *Tonight* show on TV for many years, as well as actors Al Pacino and Marlon Brando. Introverts can be as out-going and vivacious as extroverts, yet they do not draw energy from the encounter. Performance exhausts them, whereas for the extrovert, performance increases the pulse of energy.

Several years ago, one of this essay's authors, Raspa, an introvert, was conducting workshops for corporations to develop vision and mission statements. He was working with a highly extroverted partner. At the end of an eight-hour workshop, the introvert would be exhausted, aching to lie down and rest, while the extrovert was excited. At the airport standing in line to check in luggage, the introvert would be sleepy and close his eyes to shut out the world, hoping no one would talk to him, yearning to move through the line quickly so as to find a quiet place in the corner of the airport to sleep. The extrovert, however, was making new friends in the cue line, laughing and telling jokes, and deciding where to have a snack with two or three others before the plane departed. This story illustrates the contrasts between two types. Both introverts and extroverts can stand up before groups of people, conduct workshops, give speeches, have a powerful impact on an audience, move them to laughter or tears, charm them, engage them deeply in important matters. The difference: extroverts are energized by the process, introverts are tired by it.

Another quality that distinguishes the two is that for introverts, the real world is interior, "in here." It is the mind, the imagination, the flow of personal feeling and thought that compel the introvert's attention. For the extrovert, the real world is outside the self, "out there," where things happen with other people.

There are three times more extroverts in our culture than introverts. We cherish outer-directed behavior and remain somewhat suspicious of solitude. We tend to say good things about being the life of the party and are inclined to see reserved behavior as unfriendly or condescending. Much of the bias would disappear if we remember that all of us are capable of introversion or extroversion, though our experience of them will be different, and that the distinction has to do with energy rather than style of self-presentation. If we remember this, we can be more patient with ourselves and, perhaps, feel more compassion for others.

Other qualities of this scale are worth mentioning. Extroverts like to work through their ideas by talking with others. In fact, extroverts think best when they can talk aloud their thoughts, vocalizing their ruminations. If you placed tape over an extrovert's mouth, it would be difficult for that person to process information. In the classroom, introverts and extroverts are easily identified. Introverts prefer to work on ideas by themselves. Extroverts come alive in group interaction.

Research has suggested that the majority of librarians and faculty are introverts.[6] This fact carries tremendous implications for collaboration. It means that, by preference, librarians and faculty do not naturally look to work with others. More important, the preference for introversion means that librarians and faculty, who value the importance of collaboration, may need to overcome a natural resistance to this kind of relationship. We may need to stretch our ability to listen to each other in a new way.

Perhaps we need to listen to each other as we listen to ourselves. As introverts, we may need to listen to one another quietly and reflectively, building trust into the process. At the very least, we must establish congruence in our manner of communication with each other. F. R. Yeakley pointed out that "two people must use the same communication style at the same time in order to communicate effectively. This often requires some communication adjustment on the part of one or both of the individuals involved."[7] We believe the most powerful listening is what we call re-creation, re-creating what the other is saying and then restating it for confirmation. Listening as re-creation is a gift. It says to the other: you are worth listening to. You have something important to say. I value what you are thinking and feeling.

To listen in this fashion may require that we give up certain things, such as expectations of how other people should communicate or assessments of how that person or those people are, and perhaps most important, we have to give up the epistemological stance that "we already know." We already know what that person will say or do, we already know how this or that will turn out because of past precedent or simple cause and effect relationships, and because we have been around long enough to have gotten the picture of the way it is around here. Many people already know that collaboration will not work at their institution because they know how those people they work with really are.

To bring a relationship and, ultimately, collaboration alive, the authors invite you to engage in what Allen Parry and Robert Doan call "not-knowing" listening.[8] Listen to the other "as if" you have just been introduced to that person and listen as an interested observer who is open to hear what the other is thinking and feeling. Listen from the stance that you do not know. Or, to put this another way, listen for surprise. This kind of listening can break through much of the mechanical and stereotypic listening that suffocates relationships. Unfortunately, this is what many people experience as normal. Openness for surprise will delight you and create aliveness in the relationships right in front of you.

Scale 2: Assessing Information
In addition to introversion/extroversion, a second scale looks at how we prefer to assess information, through either the five senses, sensing, or through some sort of inner vision, intuiting. Sensors are generally more detail oriented and focused on what is here and now. They are comfortable with sequencing a process or idea, seeing how the parts are all connected, observing how things were done in the past, and looking for ways to extend the continuity. They are comfortable with concrete procedures and specific sequences. Past practices give a sense of order and stability. In contrast, intuitors

prefer the "big picture" and like to envision future possibilities. They are inclined to process information holistically, looking for abstract connections, theoretical underpinnings, conceptual possibilities. Intuitors see everything connected to everything else—the entire world is one continuous gossamer of energy. In an anthropology class, for instance, an intuitive instructor could bring to life the ways every culture deals with death through the phoenix paradigm, an image of endless endings and new beginnings.

Research suggests that faculty generally hold an intuitor preference, whereas librarians are equally divided between sensing and intuition. The potential for miscommunication between sensors and intuitors is tremendous. The former group may be suspicious of the continual talk of possibilities, whereas the latter may be uninspired by the ordinary quality of the real. Imagine, for a moment, that you are on a group tour with faculty and librarians, flying in a big jumbo jet airplane, cruising at 36,000 feet over the North Atlantic with 400 other passengers. Suddenly, the pilot breaks into the public address system and announces that the rudders are not working properly, and he is going to return to Rome for an emergency landing. He reassures you that there is nothing to worry about. In this emergency situation, what is required is a pilot who can follow a set of very complex procedures to maneuver the giant machine to a safe landing. We would not want the pilot to theorize the problem or deal with it abstractly. In this emergency situation, we want a sensor not an intuitor. However, if we were returning from a tour of Italy and had gone to the *Galleria Academia* in Florence to experience Michelangelo's *David*, we would want to have had a guide who could make the conceptual leap to show us the power of that grand statue. *David*'s power is universal. It is in all of us. The statue represents that time when we are faced with an overwhelming challenge that we fear is going to kill us. *David*'s stance is the moment of turning—turning away from our fear of death and calling forth the courage to face our problem. What we want in the aesthetic domain is an intuitive grasp of the connection between art and our lives, not a literal explanation of how the different parts of the statue are put together. When people grasp their connectedness to *David,* it takes their breath away. Art illuminates the hidden parts of life and gives it meaning.

Perhaps this axis of perception—sensor and intuition—is the most difficult to bridge. Sensors are impatient with the irrelevant comments of the intuitors. A common complaint is: "What does *that*—what you just said—have to do with *this*—the problem at hand. Huh? Huh? Huh?" Intuitors, on the other hand, are bored by the literal-minded quality of sensors. One usual lament is the following: "You fail to see the possibilities that are embedded in this situation because you are stuck in procedure and in linear and amazingly boring thinking!"

Although such differences challenge our patience and understanding, there are some benefits when opposites work together. As collaborators, two or more persons holding the same preference will have an easier time communicating with each other and will make decisions more quickly; however, they may not produce the best results. The theory of psychological type maintains that opposite preferences complement each other and, if sustained, will generate better outcomes. Some of the psychological distance between librarians and faculty undoubtedly results from a lack of awareness about our own preferences and those of potential collaborators. Rather than persevering in our efforts to understand and listen to each other, we jump to an unwarranted conclusion that librarians and faculty are basically incompatible. In fact, intuitors are especially strong in providing visions of new possibilities. But it is sensors who, as masters of detail, can best determine the steps in manifesting that vision and bringing it to fruition.

Scale 3: Acting on Information

The third scale of the MBTI attempts to help us clarify our decision-making process. This scale measures what we do with information after we have processed it. We prefer to make decisions either by applying an impersonal logic, thinking, or by more person-centered values, feeling. Again, thinking and feeling represent complementary processes, but the differences between them breed a great deal of misunderstanding. Thinkers are often seen as "cold" and feelers as "overly sentimental." In higher education, thinking is the dominant preference, but without an understanding of preferences, we become separated from each other by a tendency to use stereotypes. In fact, values are inherent in every decision. Feelers often provide insight into current processes and question those that leave people out of the equation. Thinkers support a value system by applying clear reasoning. In practice, confusion between thinkers and feelers occurs when the former discusses decision making within the context of an existent value system and the latter discusses decisions within the context of a changed system.

Scale 4: Facing Other People

The final scale explores our "lifestyle" orientations, which has to do with our preference for open-endedness, perceiving, or closure, judging. The scale tells us how we act on information in the world. Perceivers are comfortable keeping options open; judgers are not critical people but, rather, people who seek resolution. So the two types—one oriented to openness and the other to closure—represent the two tendencies inherent in all of us. Decision making represents a time to close off possibilities. When you have a complex decision to make, do you put it off as long as possible, preferring to gather still more data, more possibilities, to help you finally come to closure? Or are you fairly confident about your decision after you have seen some—though not all—of the evidence? When you visit Baskin-Robbins's thirty-one flavors, do you already know what flavor you will choose before you enter the store? Or do you have to use the little pink spoons to taste eight or nine different flavors, while you keep asking for more time, sheepishly inviting others waiting impatiently in line to go ahead of you so you can contemplate all the flavor possibilities? When you are completing a project, do you always need more time, even when you start out early? Or can you fit it in and complete the task no matter what?

These four scales help us understand what our natural preferences are—our ways of folding not our hands but, rather, metaphorically folding the world and the self for presentation in the world. They are not intended to label us or limit our dreams or aspirations. They are useful tools for understanding what we must do to create a successful project or engage another human being.

Within institutions of higher education, the administration and application of the Myers-Briggs Type Indicator provides us with an opportunity to develop a metadialogue, or conversation about our conversation. Its use in this way represents an invitation to listen to each other, offering us a new freedom to create networks, to break through outmoded forms of organizational relationships. We have visited university departments where the MBTI has become a part of organizational life. The members of one department at Wayne State University have even posted their Myers-Briggs type on their office doors.

COLLABORATION AND THE FLOW STATE

Another expression of new science is also from psychology. It draws on the psychological work of Mihaly Csikszentmihalyi, George Leonard, and David Steindl-Rast that deals with increasing human potential and joy in life.[9–11] This body of research raises the question, when are we most effective and joyful? and proposes that is it when we are in what Csikszentmihalyi calls the flow state. The flow state is that state of mind when everything disappears and all that remains in consciousness is the activity or person right before us. We are in the present. We lose awareness of past or future time. Csikszentmihalyi's research shows that surgeons who have been in the operating room for four or five hours, intensely concentrating on the procedure, will say when they leave the OR that they felt as though they were in the room for twenty minutes or so. Such a statement reveals further qualities of the flow state. There is no separation between ourselves and what we are doing but, rather, a merging of self and activity. In the flow state, there is a sense of effortlessness. We have the feeling of control, as our attention is fixed on a narrow range of action. Again, rock climbers Csikszentmihalyi studied feel connected to the mountain as if the mountain were an extension of the self. Tennis players, also, in the heat of a game sometimes report that the racket is an extension of their arm; they are not playing the game of tennis. They feel as though they are the game. It is the feeling the Irish poet William Butler Yeats captured in the image: "How can I know the dancer from the dance?" Where does the dancer end and the dance begin? The boundaries separating self and activity in the flow state merge. We are relaxed, our attention is focused in the here and now, our troubles are bracketed and outside consciousness, and we are poised, ready for whatever shows up—even the unexpected or surprising. Shakespeare used the expression "The readiness is all" to describe that state of being.

Can we approximate the flow state collaborating with another person? We think so. Members of a symphonic orchestra sometimes report that when the playing is very fine, they feel as though they are one rich instrument, and as they play they are lost in the music. A symphonic orchestra is an ensemble collaboration. What is required to lift such a group to inspired performance is the paradox: listening with your eyes and seeing with your ears, as one member of the Detroit Symphony reported. In other words, to increase the likelihood of entering flow with others in a group, everyone needs to concentrate all of his or her attention on the play of the moment so intensely that every sense is cooperating with every other sense in engaging the process. Can librarians and faculty achieve flow together? Yes, provided they are willing to do some things and give up others. Below is a list of actions that may induce the flow experience in a collaborative project:

• **Be present.** The single most important thing you can do is come into the here and now. That means releasing your preoccupations with the way it was or the way it might or should be. For most of us, it means that we consciously choose to bracket our worries, our fears, our disappointments, our grudges, our regrets, and turn our attention to what is right before us. Engaging the task at hand can be challenging. Sometimes we have to do that a thousand times a minute because we feel as if we are being eaten by problems and fears. But the way out of the jaw of fear is the same for everybody: release the concern with the past or the future and turn to the present.

• **Give up complaining and blaming.** Work life offers many opportunities to complain about what is not working or to blame someone or some group for it. When we are in the complaint mode, we cannot bring anything to life. We may be able to muddle through, may get some satisfaction in having projected blame and gotten it off our chest, but we have not summoned the potential energy inherent in the world when we are connected to others.

• **Chop wood and carry water.** This is Leonard's way of imaging what is required to sustain commitment to a project when you find yourself on a plateau, doing the same things again and again. The axiom is: love the plateau, learn to love the somewhat boring, but necessary, tasks that are part of every project—such as chopping wood and carrying water for survival.

These are a few of the new developments in science that shed light on the process of collaboration. The authors invite you to use these insights to extend your own power to connect and summon possibilities. "Life is either a daring adventure or nothing, " Helen Keller said. Practicing these principles can launch us on the adventure of our lives.

We remain rooted in process and relationship. Our effort to develop more collaborative relationships on campus represents the birth of a new way of working. New science reveals that a dynamically interdependent future stands before us, and our task involves learning how to work together. As a process, the application of personality instruments such as the Myers Briggs Type Indicator will facilitate our mutual growth and discovery of this new universe. Nothing less than joy and flow await us down the road.

NOTES

1. Alvin Toffler, *The Third Wave* (New York: Morrow, 1980).

2. Margaret Wheatley, *Leadership and the New Science: Learning about Organization from an Orderly Universe* (San Francisco: Berrett-Koehler, 1992): 38.

3. Ibid., 32.

4. Ibid.

5. Ibid., 7.

6. For teachers and faculty, see Gordon Lawrence, *People Types & Tiger Stripes* (Gainesville, Fla.: Center for Applications of Psychological Type, 1996), 71-86. For librarians, see Mary Jane Scherdin, "Vive la Différence: Exploring Librarian Personality Types Using the MBTI," in *Discovering Librarians: Profiles of a Profession*, ed. Mary Jane Scherdin (Chicago: ACRL, 1994): 126–56.

7. F. R. Yeakley, "Implications of Communications Style Research for Psychological Type Theory," *Research in Psychological Type* 6 (1983): 5.

8. Allan Parry and Robert Doan, *Story Revisions: Narrative Therapy in the Postmodern World* (London: Guilford Pr., 1994).

9. See, for example, Mihaly Csikszentmihalyi, *Flow: The Psychology of Optimal Experience* (New York: Harper & Row, 1990); ———, *Finding Flow: The Psychology of Engagement with Everyday Life* (New York: Basic Bks., 1997); ———, *Creativity: Flow and the Psychology of Discovery and Invention* (New York: HarperCollins, 1996).

10. George Leonard, *Mastery* (New York: Dutton, 1991).

11. David Steindl-Rast, *Gratefulness, the Heart of Prayer* (New York: Paulist Pr., 1984).

Collaborations in the Field: Examples from a Survey

Bee Gallegos
Arizona State University West

Thomas Wright
Brigham Young University

Everywhere, librarians and faculty are collaborating on exciting projects that sparkle with creativity and synergy. In recent years, we have discovered some marvelous initiatives that provoked us to find other models. We were particularly interested in those projects undertaken by individual librarians and classroom faculty, as opposed to those initiated at an institutional level. What types of projects do librarians and faculty pursue, we wondered? Subsequently during late 1998, we solicited model projects with a survey posted to numerous electronic discussions, most of them affiliated with the Association of College and Research Libraries (ACRL). The focus of these discussions covered a wide area of librarianship, including subject specializations, collection development, and library instruction. In brief, the survey attempted to discover the details of collaborative projects, as well as their development, impact, and future prospects. What were the common characteristics of these projects? In the end, we received fifty-three surveys. Of those, fifty-one came from the United States, one from Australia, and one from Canada.

Concerned that respondents might be unfamiliar with the distinction between *collaboration* and other, related terms, we included a definition from the 1996 publication, *Collaboration*, by Robert Grover and the American Association of School Librarians (AASL).[1] Here, collaboration was defined as a more intensive and integrated working relationship than those relationships characterized by *cooperation* and *coordination*. We hoped to find examples of librarians and faculty who were working, teaching, and writing "out of the box," who had stepped beyond departmental walls to create powerful projects.

OVERVIEW OF FINDINGS

We learned a great deal about the practice of collaboration from this survey of our colleagues. For instance, we discovered— somewhat to our surprise—that most of these projects revolved around instruction. Approximately 60 percent of the surveys described an instructional collaboration. Other project areas included collection building, Web page design, curricular revision, faculty–staff development, grant writing, publications, and conference presentations. Several initiatives did not begin with the end result in mind, which demonstrated that collaboration is a process that continues to evolve along with the interpersonal relationships of the participants. We also noted that many of these projects resulted in presentations and publications that reached a broad, interdisciplinary audience.

As a whole, the surveys yielded several lessons about the process of collaboration. First, working relationships are based on issues of mutual concern. Therefore, potential collaborators must engage each other in real conversation about those topics that interest and inspire them. Second, they must be able and willing to propose a joint project and then to initiate a process of exploration. This requires participants to listen to each other in an attentive, trusting, and respectful manner. It involves exploring the collaborative process of playing with ideas. Third, the manner in which collaborators work together has a great deal to do with particular preferences. This may take some time and negotiation but should not be taken for granted. The process of working together requires discussion.

The following list of twelve projects, laboriously gleaned from a fine collection of collaborative endeavors, provides useful insights into the nature and variety of librarian–faculty collaboration. Perhaps most important, they reveal that powerful projects can only succeed when we take the small risk of stepping out of our comfort zones. In the pages that follow, you will read of colleagues who found commitment in each other for a common goal and, ultimately, greater mutual understanding and appreciation.

CASE STUDIES IN SCIENCE: A WORKSHOP AND NATIONAL CLEARINGHOUSE

This ambitious collaborative project from the State University of New York at Buffalo has been designed to help undergraduate science faculty teach with active learning techniques, especially case studies. It features a grant-funded, five-day workshop on case study methodology and a Web site created as a national clearinghouse for case studies in science. The collaborators and codirectors of the project are Nancy A. Schiller, associate librarian, Science and Engineering Library, and Clyde F. Herreid, distinguished teaching professor, Biological Sciences Department.

The project originated with Herreid and Schiller as coprincipal investigators of a two-year $119,000 Undergraduate Faculty Enhancement program grant from the National Science Foundation's Division of Undergraduate Education. In that role, they organize the workshop and maintain the Web site (http://ublib.buffalo.edu/libraries/projects/cases) with the help of a quarter-time librarian. Attendees of the all-expenses-paid workshop are expected to write a case for the case study collection within six months of the workshop. Several participants have written articles on the technique for science education journals.

Possible future funding from a major private philanthropic organization may permit Herreid and Schiller to offer two workshops each year, which would include a series of videotapes on the case method for teaching undergraduate science courses.

CORE-CHEMISTRY/OHIOLINK RESOURCE EXPLORER

At Youngstown State University, a group of librarians and faculty created a chemistry Web site that incorporated syllabi, class assignments, interactive chemistry problem sets, and links to library resources. In the process, the two groups developed a strong working relationship that had not previously existed.

Collaborators included Lee-Ann McAllister and Catherine Cardwell, assistant reference librarians; and Tom Kim and Peter Norris, assistant professors of chemistry, Youngstown State University. (Cardwell has since become library instruction coordinator at Bowling Green State University.) The project began with an inquiry to chemistry faculty concerning their interest in submitting a collaborative grant proposal to design an instructional/ research Web site. All members of the group subsequently contributed to the proposal, which was submitted to OhioLink, a statewide library consortium. After obtaining the grant, each member took responsibility for the development of various components of the site. The librarians provided links to subject-specific resources and databases, coupled with strategies for conducting research. They worked closely with a graphic arts student to design the Web site. Chemistry faculty included course-specific materials, links to general chemistry sites, and interactive course work (http://iws.ohiolink.edu/chemistry/).

The project began with a first meeting in January 1998. They received the grant in April and opened the site in September. The group held weekly meetings throughout this period. "Librarian collaboration with chemistry faculty allowed the information needs of the students and faculty to be better understood and evaluated," according to the survey.

In the aftermath of this project, the library experienced greater use of its resources by chemistry students. Future plans include the establishment of a library liaison to the chemistry department.

A Course on Women and Western Culture

At the University of Arizona, a librarian and a classroom faculty member have teamed up to develop innovative writing assignments for the Women and Western Culture course that require students to conduct research, create group Web pages, evaluate Web sites, and participate in an electronic discussion.

Ruth Dickstein, social sciences librarian, and Kari McBride, lecturer in the women's studies department, worked together to design assignments, and provide support so that students could master the research and writing skills. Their close work together is reflected in their carefully constructed Web site (http://wwwu.arizona.edu/ic/mcbride/ws200.htm).

As in other collaborations, Dickstein and McBride are continuing to work together and currently are planning a teaching partnership for the Gender and Contemporary Society course. For more information, contact Ruth Dickstein at <dickstei@bird.library.arizona.edu>.

Creating an Information Literacy Workbook and Web Activities

This project at California State University-Chico, involved three individuals teaching a first-year experience course called Introduction to University Life. The collaborators developed a course workbook incorporating the teaching of information and computer competencies, and subsequently began working on Web-based lab activities.

The project began in 1996 with the decision to pilot a freshman orientation course, 50 percent of which was to focus on information literacy. The collaborators included Jim Owens, associate professor of management; Lori Dixon, associate professor of construction management; and Sarah Blakeslee, information literacy/instruction librarian. At one point, Owens asked Blakeslee and Dixon to help design and teach the information and computer skills component of the course. Agreeing that the course required more integration of information literacy, they decided to write the text.

The collaborators have received two grants, completed two editions of the student information literacy workbook (required in all seventeen sections) presented at two local conferences, and given a paper at the Students in Transition Conference in Irvine, California. Currently, they are working on a grant to create web-based activities for the course. They meet at least once a week to brainstorm, plan, write, and develop the Web site (http://infocomp.csuchico.edu). Their work has resulted in strong working friendships that allow them to have fun while developing products to improve teaching. For further information, contact Sarah Blakeslee at <SBLAKESLEE@scuchico.edu>.

Developing an Informatics Skills Course

At the University of Arizona, librarians and instructional faculty collaborated to create a course that helps future pharmacists and nurses become proficient in retrieving, managing, evaluating, and presenting information to colleagues, patients, and staff.

Many individuals from the Health Sciences Library, the College of Pharmacy, and the College of Nursing collaborated to create Pharmacy Practice 417: The Internet—An Introduction to Application and Use. These included librarians Mari J. Stoddard, head of educational services, Fred Heidenreich, and Hannah M. Fisher; pharmacy faculty Theodore Tong, director of the Arizona Poison Control System; Timothy Wunz, director of information technology; John Gilkey, specialist in faculty development; and nursing colleague, Beverly Rosenthal, coordinator of the Learning Resources Center.

The project began in 1995 with a meeting of Stoddard, Tong, Heidenreich, and Wunz to decide what would be taught and by whom. In practice, the three institutional role players have divided responsibilities. The library provides instruction on information retrieval, management, and assessment. The College of Pharmacy maintains a list of relevant Web sites and delivers instruction on graphics software and presentation design. The College of Nursing provides instructional software and computing support.

The course has been very successful, judging by pre- and posttest evaluation, faculty and peer appraisal of projects, and student evaluations of faculty and content. "Student evaluation is enthusiastic," according to the survey response, "and the number of students wishing to take the elective increases each year…Two students based their theses on elective projects." The pharmacy course provided a model for another in the College of Nursing. As the courses evolved, they incorporated Web design, the role of health providers in disseminating information, and participation on institutional informatics teams. By 1999, the two courses were merged and offered to students in both pharmacy and nursing (http://www.pharmacy.arizona.edu/417/index.html). "Collaboration between library and academic faculty brings strengths of both disciplines to information skills courses." For more information, contact Mari Stoddard at <stoddard@ahsl.arizona.edu>.

INSTRUCTIONAL COLLABORATION LEADS TO OTHER PROJECTS

A project at Arizona State University West demonstrates that working together on campus frequently leads to other types of collaboration, including publications and presentations. Bee Gallegos, education librarian, and Peter Rillero, assistant professor in science education, found that their knowledge and experiences complemented each other. Rillero formerly worked as an educational analyst for ERIC and was well versed in the technical aspects of the database. Gallegos was experienced in searching ERIC. Similar to other projects presented here, this one showed that the initial step of discovering common interests is critical to the pursuit of any collaborative endeavor.

Gallegos and Rillero began their work together by coteaching a session of his Science and Social Studies Methods class, with each of them taking responsibility for various points. Following this, the collaborators discussed the need to identify and further refine the core competencies students need to qualify as successful researchers of information. They agreed that these competencies would provide a framework around which their collaborative instructional sessions would focus. Their continued work resulted in a local conference presentation, as well as a publication in *The Journal of Technology and Teacher Education*. Over time, these collaborators discovered a style of working together that suited them both, based on openness, trust, and division of labor.

The project resulted in requests from other faculty interested in developing and applying a core set of research competencies. For more information, contact Bee Gallegos at <Bee.Gallegos@asu.edu>.

LITERATURE-BASED SOCIAL STUDIES AT BRIGHAM YOUNG UNIVERSITY

This project, involving Brigham Young University education librarian Thomas C. Wright and education professor Lynnette Erickson, consisted of producing a K–3 literature-based social studies curriculum for the Provo, Utah, school district.

Like so many other collaborative undertakings, this one began with the discovery of mutual interests, which provided a foundation for their future work. With an interest in social studies and children's literature, Wright and Erickson found that their skills also complemented each other. Erickson used knowledge of social studies curriculum and connections in local schools to initiate the work, while Wright assisted in book selection and the writing/editing of materials. In sum, the collaborators produced the curriculum with books purchased by the school district and workshops presented on their use.

Wright and Erickson have submitted an article for publication on this project and have delivered several presentations at the conference of the National Council for the Social Studies. For further information, contact Thomas Wright at <tom_wright@byu.edu>.

SANTA CLARA UNIVERSITY'S DIVERSITY WEB SITE PROJECT

In this collaborative initiative, two faculty members and a librarian collaborated to create a Web site of local ethnic resources to provide information and teaching resources to a variety of constituencies, including the core curriculum, the Freshman Residential

Community, the Ethnic Studies Program, and community users. The neighboring city of San Jose is 24 percent Hispanic, 23 percent Asian, and 4 percent African American. The Diversity Project provides universal access—through the Internet—to the cultural richness of the Silicon Valley, while supporting a multicultural emphasis in the curriculum of Santa Clara University.

The project resulted from the merging of two related, though organizationally distinct, initiatives. Faculty members Stephen S. Fugita, director of ethnic studies, and Eric Hanson, director of the core curriculum committee, had been participants in a committee discussing the creation of a database of Silicon Valley ethnicity. At the same time, librarian Aimee Algier, head of serials and ethnic studies specialist, had been working on a broadly conceived Web site of diversity resources. After becoming aware of each other's work, they joined forces. Fugita and Hanson obtained money for the project, including a grant from the James Irvin Foundation, while Algier planned and directed it. She hired students to search the Internet and newspapers and phonebooks for ethnic resources such as organizations and cultural centers. The students subsequently wrote brief essays about each resource and provided graphics for the Santa Clara University Web site.

The site has succeeded in becoming an active part of the curriculum and community. Students in the Freshman Residential Community continue to add Web pages, Ethnic Studies classes explore the site for assignments, and others use it to help fulfill a United States course requirement in university core curriculum. E-mail to the *San Jose Mercury News* indicates that the community makes good use of the Web site. It has achieved two Snap Online "Best of the Web" awards and a University Staff Recognition Award. Plans include enhancing the site with articles on the Chicano farm labor movement in the Valley (www.scu.edu/SCU/Programs/Diversity/homepage. html). For more information, contact <Aimee Algier at AAlgier@scu.edu>.

Teaching Research: A Workshop for Instructors and Librarians

At the University of Kansas, two librarians obtained a grant from a funding source on campus to develop and deliver a collaborative workshop concerning the effective teaching of library research skills. During the workshop, ten teaching faculty were paired with library staff to jointly explore creation of library activities for one of their classes.

Cindy Pierard, library instruction coordinator, and Mary Rosenbloom, reference librarian/women's studies bibliographer, obtained the necessary funding and managed the project. Classroom faculty agreed to participate in the workshop and to partner with library staff in the planning and implementation of library-related components. During the workshop, participants discussed how the teaching of library research could facilitate the achievement of other pedagogical objectives. In addition, faculty agreed to submit course materials to the project Web site (http://www2.lib.ukans.edu/ ~instruction/ special_projects/) and to act as resource people for the campus teaching community.

The workshop provided a forum through which librarians and teaching faculty could develop successful partnerships, resulting in more effective library research instruction and assignments. Future revisions of the workshop may focus specifically on teams of library subject specialists and teaching faculty. For more information, contact Cindy Pierard at <cpierard@mail.lib.ukans.edu>.

Teaching Research with a Web-Based Chemistry Internet Assignment

A librarian and chemistry instructor at Pennsylvania State University, Lehigh Valley, collaborated to create a Web-based instruction module that teaches students how to conduct research with chemistry resources on the Internet. The close relationship between collaborators Renee Gittler, senior lecturer in chemistry, and Judy Lichtman, reference librarian, is reflected in the careful construction of the Web site.

Gittler initiated the project and, in practice, provides Lichtman with information on useful chemistry topics and Web sites. Lichtman designed the assignment based on their mutual understanding of goals and objectives. The Web page has been updated each semester, most recently to give more directions to novice users (http://www.lv.psu.edu/_jkl1/chem15). Lichtman supports students through e-mail while Gittler makes herself available to students on campus. Additional interaction between students and Lichtman has been facilitated by a brief visit to the classroom earlier in the semester.

The project's success speaks for itself. Lichtman has taken the basic design and objectives of the chemistry Web site as a model for collaboration with other departments. She is currently working with English faculty to create a business writing site and has tentative plans to undertake a project about World War II. Gittler has shown the site to faculty at the main University Park campus who are considering modeling it as part of the freshman seminar. For more information, contact Judy Lichtman at <jkl1@psu.edu>.

THE TRANSFORMATION PROJECT: AN INTEGRATED WRITING AND RESEARCH PROJECT

From George Mason University's New Century College, this creative project demonstrates how library and research skills can be incorporated into an innovative "learning community" of collaboratively taught course work. Through a series of activities completed over the course of a year, the Transformation Project provides freshmen the opportunity to develop their research, writing, and technology skills.

In practice, each student chooses a person to study throughout the year and completes four research and writing activities or "chapters," focused specifically on the theme of each learning community. For instance, students may research the social context of an individual's activities for a sociology component of the learning community. At the end of the year, students write an analysis and reflective piece for their portfolio.

Jim Young, New Century College liaison librarian, acts as project manager for the faculty working group that includes Leslie Smith, English; Ashley Williams, composition; Tom Wood, biology; Jim Barry, public policy; and Kelly Dunne, New Century College. This group plays a leading role in the design and implementation of the project, and maintains its Web site (http://mason.gmu.edu/~jyoung/transformation). The integrated nature of this project—and the fact that students participate in the learning community as a cohort—means that librarians, faculty, and students establish real relationships during the year and feel ownership for the program. For more information, contact Jim Young at <jyoung8@gmu.edu>.

WRITING BOOKS ON WORLD WIDE WEB RESEARCH

At Mary Washington College, Karen Hartman, reference and bibliographic enstruction librarian, and Ernest Ackermann, professor of computer science, have collaborated in writing several books concerning research on the Web. Their work together has grown to include presentations and workshops at national conferences.

Their first endeavor, initiated by Ackermann, involved writing a book called *Searching and Researching on the Internet and the World Wide Web*. Hartman created a book outline in the summer of 1996, and both of them worked on a proposal that called for an equal number of chapters from the authors. They contacted publisher Franklin, Beedle and Associates and signed a contract to begin the book in November 1996. Published in December 1997, the book was so successful that it resulted in a revised edition the following year. A second book, called *Internet and Web Essentials* was, at the time of this writing, scheduled for publication sometime at the end of 1999.

Similar to the experience of other collaborators, Ackermann and Hartman saw their work continue to grow into related projects. "The collaboration has turned into an ongoing working relationship," they write. Besides their second book, they provided a workshop at WebNet 98 and a presentation at EDUCOM 1998.

In addition, they learned about their colleague's perspective. "The best part about this collaboration was learning about information and computer technology from a nonlibrarian's viewpoint," says Hartman. For more information, contact Karen Hartman at <khartman@mwc.edu>.

NOTE

1. Robert Grover, *Collaboration* (Chicago: American Association of School Librarians, 1996).

APPENDIX A
OTHER PROJECTS

Name of Project	Type	Institution	Contact
Guided Autobiographical Writing	Instruction	Wayne State University	Sally Lawler Ad5748@ wayne.edu
Biography Class	Instruction	Santa Clara University	Gail Gradowski Ggradowski@ scu.edu
English 108: Academic Writing	Instruction	Marygrove College	Linnea Dudley ldudley@ marygrove.edu
Summer Library Faculty Workshop	Instruction	Hanover College	Laurel A. Carter Laurel.Whisler@ furman.edu
A Scavenger Hunt: An Exercise in Collaboration	Instruction	Moravian College	Bonnie Falla Fallab@ moravian.edu
Core/ID 106 (Global Issues) Library Component	Instruction	Moravian College	Linda M. LaPointe lapointe@ moravian.edu
Enhancing Research Skills with WWW and Traditional Tools	Instruction and research	Miami University	Joanne M. Goode jgoode@lib. muohio.edu
Humanities on the Internet	Instruction	Weber State University	Carol Hanson Chansen@ weber.edu
Research Consultant	Research	University of Melbourne	Sabina Robertson s.robertson@lib. unimelb.edu.au
Liaison Program	Research University	Northwestern State	Martha V. Henderson Henderson@ nsula.edu
American Language Program	Instruction	California State University	John Hickok Jhickok@ fullerton.edu
Library Skills and Research in Women's Studies	Instruction	University of Maine	Nancy M. Lewis Nancy_Lewis@ umit.maine.edu

Name of Project	Type	Institution	Contact
Medical Informatics Clerkship	Instruction	Indiana University School of Medicine	Sue London Slondon@ iupui.edu
School of Pharmacy Curriculum Revision	Curricular revision/ collection development	School of Pharmacy University of the Pacific	Kimberly Lyons klyons@uop.edu
Bibliographic Instruction	Instruction	University of the Pacific	Kimberly Lyons klyons@uop.edu
Library Remodel	Grant writing	University of the Pacific	Kimberly Lyons klyons@uop.edu
Globalizing Environmental Education	Instruction	South Dakota State University	Nancy Marshall Marshaln@mg. sdstate.edu
Composition 130: Introductory Writing in the Natural Sciences	Instruction	Colgate University	Debbie Huerta dhuerta@MAIL. COLGATE.EDU
Preparations for Library Instruction Sessions	Instruction	Maryville College	Roger Myers myers@ maryvillecollege.edu
Graduate Research Methods Course in English	Instruction	University of New Orleans	Jeanne Pavy jpavy@uno.edu
Biologist's Guide to Library Resources	Instruction	Tufts University	Regina Fisher Raboin Rraboin@infonet. tufts.edu
Bibliography/Joint Publication	Publication	University of Waterloo	Shabiran Rahman srahman@library. uwaterloo.ca
Library 140: Special Topics in Information Literacy	Instruction	University of Rhode Island	Andree J. Rathemacher andree@uri.edu
Engelond (Web-based resource)	Instruction/ research	Ohio State University	Scott Walter walter.123@osu.edu
Tennessee Nurse Practitioner's Information Literacy	Research	East Tennessee State University	Rosalee J. Seymour Seymourr@etsu.edu
Increasing and Managing Spanish-Language Pedagogical Resources and Children's Books	Collection development and collection management	Arizona State University	Bee Gallegos Bee.Gallegos@ asu.edu

Name of Project	Type	Institution	Contact
Evaluation of WWW Resources	Instruction	University of Richmond	Lucretia McCulley lmcculle@ richmond.edu
Freshman Orientation Online Scavenger Hunt	Instruction	University of Connecticut	Shelley Cudiner s.cudiner@ uconn.edu
University Library Faculty Workshop on Geographic Information Systems (GIS)	Instruction	Old Dominion University	Stuart Frazer Sfrazer@odu.edu
Literature Review Paper: A Collaborative Approach to Integrating Library Research into Psychology Courses	Instruction	Moravian College	Bonnie Falla Fallab@ moravian.edu
Education 376: Whose School is It Anyway?	Instruction	Millersville University	Robert Coley Rcoley@marauder. millersv.edu
Online Reference and Chat Rooms in Support of English Composition	Instruction	Southeastern Louisiana University	Barbara D'Angelo bdangelo@asu.edu
Reforming Higher Education to Serve Hispanic Students	Grant proposal/ collection development	California State University, Fresno	Mike Tillman miket@ csufresno.edu
Health Information Access for Rural Nurse Practitioners	Instruction	Six Minnesota colleges and universities	Karla Block Karla.J.Block-2@ tc.umn.edu
Community College Leadership Distance Program	Instruction	Oregon State University	Jean Caspers Jean.caspers@ orst.edu
Faculty/Librarian Team Teaching of Information Literacy Survival Skills	Instruction	University of Connecticut	Shelley Cudiner s.cudiner@ uconn.edu
ArkMOO	Reference/ Instruction	Arizona State University West, University of Arkansas at Little Rock	Barbara J. D'Angelo bdangelo@asu.edu
University of Iowa Information Initiative (UTriplel)	Instruction	University of Iowa	Carol A. Hughes
Updating, Revamping, and Enhancing the Health Sciences and Chemistry Library	Collection Development	University of the Pacific	Kimberly Lyons klyons@uop.edu

Name of Project	Type	Institution	Contact
Teacher as Scholar, Student Teaching Seminar	Instruction	St. Mary's College of Maryland	Celia Rabinowitz erabinowitz@ osprey.smcm.edu
Finding Resources in Criminology and Criminal Justice: A Web-Based Tutorial	Instruction	Western Michigan University	Patricia Vander Meer pat.vandermeer@ wmich.edu

The Librarian as Networker: Setting the Standard for Higher Education

Shellie Jeffries
Wayne State University

The most pedestrian view of librarians is that they answer questions, help members of a local community find books, and then spend the rest of their time sitting quietly at their desks reading. Even at colleges and universities, librarians are often seen as helpers, those who assist inexperienced people navigate through the library—locating the appropriate books, serials, videos, microfiche, reference materials, and, perhaps most important, electronic resources.

Because of our position in the academic environment, we librarians have an opportunity to influence education by networking with faculty. When librarians participate in robust partnerships with faculty, their role as agents of educational transformation is brought to life. Librarians have the potential to affect the evolution of the academy as it moves into next millennium.

Collaboration between librarians and faculty will change as the electronic universe creates opportunities to (net)work together. Electronic information has become the medium in which people do research, write papers, learn, and even demonstrate mastery of a subject area. Survival in the new millennium will depend on those who can use information electronically. Librarians are on the edge of the information explosion and play a critical role in educating citizens about effective use of technology.

This essay discusses the role of the librarian as networking agent. Its orientation is practical, providing suggestions for developing relationships with faculty. It is based on two recent surveys. One, addressed to librarians, asked questions about their experiences working and communicating with faculty. The other, directed to faculty, inquired about their perceptions of librarian–faculty collaboration and explored their preferences about the nature of those collaborative efforts. Both surveys were sent to the EBSS-L and BI-L electronic discussions. Interested librarians were asked to forward the faculty survey to those instructors whom they felt might be receptive to responding. All respondents were asked to reply via e-mail, though some written responses were sent in.

Twenty-one librarian surveys and twenty-one faculty surveys were received. The faculty responses came from a total of ten different institutions distributed across the country fairly evenly. In terms of size, four of those institutions have a student body of fewer than 11,000. Nine of them are undergraduate and graduate institutions; one is a community college. Four are located in urban areas, and six are residential colleges and universities.

The librarian responses were distributed over a wider selection of institutions, with twenty different colleges and universities represented: nineteen undergraduate and graduate institutions and, again, one community college. Geographically, nine of the institutions are located in the Midwest, with 6 in the East, two in the West, three in the South, and one in New Zealand. Six of these institutions have an enrollment of 11,000 or fewer. Seven are located in urban areas and fifteen of the twenty consist of residential schools.

The low number of responses cautions us to restrain making wide inferences. Rather, the surveys express the views of a small, but vocal and collaboratively active, minority. The results are biased toward librarians and faculty who have had effective collaborative experiences. Still, although they cannot be construed as authoritative or comprehensive, the surveys present helpful advice on librarian–faculty collaboration.

Ten Tips for Collaborating

When asked what kinds of things librarians can do to develop and enhance good working relationships with faculty, both librarians and faculty responded with practical suggestions that could lay the groundwork for more robust collaboration, such as developing a syllabus or team teaching a course.

These suggestions were:

1.   **Be interested in faculty research.** Show an interest in what the faculty member is researching or doing in the classroom. Ask questions and use every contact—at the reference desk, on the phone, in the classroom—as an opportunity to find out more about your faculty.

2.   **Be friendly.** Maintaining a positive attitude can be serendipidous and open the door to a relationship, even when a faculty member seems aloof and unapproachable.

3.   **Be courteous and respectful.** All interactions with faculty and students should express your interest in their questions and your concern about their academic success. Treat them as you want to be treated.

4.   **Be a promoter of new products, services, and acquisitions.** Be willing to demonstrate the library's new resources to faculty; many cannot keep up with the latest information technology innovations and your support will be welcome. Send them information you feel would interest them.

5.   **Be a personal librarian.** This means that you tailor your service for the individual faculty member as opposed to serving everybody in the same way. One method is to communicate ways to make the faculty workload and research easier. Another is to make it easy to obtain Web access to information for a particular course or assignment. There are many other possibilities for personalizing service as well.

6. **Be willing to attend faculty meetings.** In addition, be willing to serve on college committees and participate in other campus activities.

7. **Be committed.** Develop a reputation as someone who is reliable and never promise to do something you cannot do. Make it clear you are committed to the success of the projects you undertake.

8. **Be a good listener.** Listen enthusiastically. There is so much boredom and cynicism in educational institutions that a bright, energetic person can be an oasis of possibilities, a sanctuary for restoring faculty to their original passion for their subject. Arrange individual meetings with professors to discuss library issues. Try to understand the environment in which faculty are working and how that affects what they do. Offer suggestions for doing things together. Be open to suggestions for new ways of doing things. Emphasize the success of past collaborations. When communicating with faculty, stress how effective previous collaborative efforts have been and how you anticipate that future efforts also will be successful. Describe how future collaborations will meet a shared goal, such as student success in an academic environment.

9. **Be responsive to student needs.** If many students have the same questions, contact the professor to offer library instruction or other collaborative assistance to help students.

10. **Be knowledgeable.** The suggestion that will have the farthest-reaching effect is to know what research and professional interests your faculty have. From this knowledge, you can develop a variety of more complex collaborative interactions beyond simple informational mailings and one-shot instruction sessions. Knowing what faculty are interested in will allow you not only to better serve their needs, but also to find those whose interests correspond with your own. Then you are in a position to establish a relationship based on shared interests and expand that relationship into collaborative work, such as writing an article, making joint conference presentations, teaching a class, or developing a course.

Preferred Method of Communication Is Electronic

Several survey questions asked about the preferred methods of contacting faculty. Interestingly, whereas librarians mentioned letters, phone, faculty meetings, direct, face-to-face contact, and, mostly, e-mail, sixteen out of the twenty-one faculty (80%) preferred email for brief messages, with phone calls a distant second. If librarians have a lot of information to discuss, several faculty preferred newsletters, letters, or memos.

One rule of thumb to keep in mind when responding to a faculty member who contacts you is to use whatever communication form they used. So if a professor e-mails you, respond via e-mail.

Talking to Another Professional

Knowing how to initially address faculty members with whom you hope to establish relationships requires tact. Some institutions distinguish between "Professor" and "Dr.," whereas others are quite informal. Where librarians fit into the hierarchy of that institution also can have an effect on how to address faculty.

Survey responses from both librarians and faculty generally stated that during an initial contact, if one is not introduced by a third party (an interaction that would presumably indicate a preferred address), faculty members prefer a formal title to be used. Whether librarians move to a less formal method of address depends on several variables, such as:

• **Institutional culture:** How formal is your school? Do faculty address each other by titles?

• **Nature of your relationship with faculty:** Do you work together closely? collaborate on projects? If so, you will probably feel comfortable using first names.

• **Preference of the faculty member:** Even if you work frequently with a professor, she may prefer to be addressed by her title.

• **Your status within the institution:** If you have faculty status, you may feel that you are on equal footing and can dispense with titles early on.

If you are unsure of a particular faculty member's official title, especially if your institution employs adjunct faculty, try to find out by contacting his or her department. If that is not an option, using "Professor" is appropriate.

In some cases, a faculty member will address you by your first name. Should this happen, it is appropriate to respond by using his or her first name. However, when teaching an instruction session or otherwise working with a professor and her class, address the instructor in the same manner the class does.

BEST TIMES TO CONTACT FACULTY

When is the most convenient time to communicate with a faculty member so that you have his or her attention and interest? For the most part, librarians and faculty agreed that before classes begin or at the beginning of a semester is the best time for contact. Although many librarians specifically mentioned that after finals was not a good time, six out of fifteen faculty respondents who expressed a preference indicated that postfinals was one of the best times to communicate with them. Librarians have considered faculty to be extremely busy and unavailable after finals, but it would be worthwhile to investigate contacting faculty then.

FACILITATING COLLABORATION

When asked about proactive measures to facilitate collaboration, faculty and librarians reinforced the suggestions for enhancing relationships listed above: keep in touch via e-mail; be friendly, helpful, and informative; attend meetings; keep communication open; and so on. A recurring theme was that by doing these things, positive word of mouth would spread about the librarian's abilities, thus attracting even more requests for collaboration.

Despite some overlap with the previous suggestions, two important points were made about facilitating collaboration. One was not to worry about the people who are resistant to collaboration. They may come around eventually when they see the positive benefits of librarian–faculty collaboration.

The second was that a librarian should have a specific proposal to present to a potential collaborator. One respondent wrote that "the librarian should be willing to adjust and modify that proposal, of course, but a concrete, well-designed, carefully thought-out plan would be much more likely to be considered seriously than a vague suggestion of getting together and 'doing something.'" This is especially important when attempting to go beyond the traditional arenas of collaboration, such as library instruction or collection development, to develop a complex collaborative enterprise, such as team teaching.

Types of Collaboration and What Has Worked

For the purposes of this survey, collaboration was described as including the following: one-shot BI sessions; team teaching; developing a course syllabus and/or curriculum; developing assignments; research and writing; grant writing; presentations, seminars, workshops and conference planning; Web site development; university committees; and collection development. Although most librarians are seemingly open to collaboration of all varieties, the collaboration that actually occurs is relatively "low level." That is, it tends to be short term and somewhat fleeting, and usually involves some form of library instruction.

In fact, library instruction was the type of collaboration mentioned most frequently by librarians. Respondents emphasized the need to communicate clearly with faculty about their needs and expectations for an instructional session. Several also stressed the importance of the instructor's presence at the session to signal the importance of the session to the students.

The second most frequent form of collaboration cited by librarians involved developing Web pages for specific classes, based on suggestions from faculty. Other ideas included team teaching classes with professors; guest lecturing; demonstrating certain techniques relevant to the course, such as storytelling and book talking for teachers; and cosponsoring an annual conference, such as one in which a librarian worked with a faculty member on a reading and language arts conference.

Faculty responses varied. One respondent mentioned that he "would be tremendously flattered to be approached by a librarian seeing [as] that person could help me with my research." Most, however, seemed to be happy with announcements about library services and new developments. Several discussed approaches to collaboration that show creativity and "thinking outside the box." These included:

• librarians meeting with faculty candidates who come for onsite interviews, showing them available resources and services;

• faculty providing librarians with syllabi, proposed topics, and required materials at the beginning of the term so librarians can plan for materials and services well in advance;

• library-sponsored receptions for departmental representatives featuring wine, fruit, cheese and crackers.

Although these types of collaborations are still in the infrequent category, they could establish a foundation on which to build more robust collaborative relationships.

Lastly, one professor stressed that librarians should focus on practical applications of library resources, rather than on theory. Another urged that librarians make sure that what they teach corresponds to the needs of the class, the assignment, and the expectations of the professor. Again, these statements reinforce the notion that good communication is an essential aspect of collaboration.

Faculty responses to the question, What types of collaboration are you interested in or would be useful to you? focused primarily on library instruction, Web page development and collection development. Many professors were interested in having their students—and themselves—learn about library resources and sophisticated research strategies, but some seemed unaware that they could ask a librarian to assist them. Several described Web pages they would like to see created for their courses and a few mentioned that they appreciated being a part of collection development or knowing about the library's new acquisitions in their field. Only one specified something deeper, suggesting coteaching and developing assignments. None mentioned what might be considered major forms of collaboration, such as course development, grant writing, or conference presentations.

MAKING THE UNINTERESTED INTERESTED

When interest is not always as obvious, librarians need to be assertive. Contacting faculty directly, with a specific proposal in mind, is one method recommended by the respondents. The contact can be a face-to-face meeting, via a letter or e-mail, or by a cold call. The faculty member's response to your proposal will definitely indicate whether he or she is interested in pursuing a collaborative effort. If you receive no response, that too is a clue. Moreover, faculty responses to general publicity will signify whether they want to work with you.

Similar advice is given to those who want to encourage interest in the library and the services it offers. The respondents suggested cold calls, e-mail or letters. Several mentioned that they would contact a faculty member and offer their services when the reference desk staff gets a rash of the same questions about a course assignment. Word of mouth is a powerful persuader. Therefore, maintaining positive interactions and open communication is advised.

DEVELOPING EFFECTIVE ASSIGNMENTS

When asked whether they would be interested in working with a librarian to develop effective assignments or revise assignments that are not evoking the response they want, an overwhelming number of the faculty respondents (76%) said yes to both. Only two respondents indicated they were interested in neither. Many faculty expressed faith in librarians' ability to provide effective instruction about appropriate resources. One did state, though, that the "librarian can offer support but should allow the professor to initiate."

Librarians made several suggestions about developing effective research components of class assignments. These included:

• "Appeal to the interest of the faculty in making students better researchers."

- "Obviously, something positive, rather than negative. And stated with enthusiasm. Maybe something like: 'Have you considered having your students do…? I can see that it might be an effective way for them to develop their critical thinking skills. I read an interesting article (heard an interesting presentation, talked to a colleague at another institution about an interesting idea) that described a class assignment that was quite innovative in its research components. If you're interested, maybe we could work on adapting it for one of your classes.'"

- "Phrases such as 'Have you considered using/doing … as an alternative approach for this assignment?' or 'Are you aware that we now have … database/resource/etc.…available at the library and having your students learn how to use this would be helpful? I can assist you in finding ways to incorporate this into your current assignment.'"

- "The only time I've contacted faculty about their library assignments is when there are typos, really glaring mistakes in instruction, or our resources have changed in some manner. I haven't spoken to them about changing the way they ask their students to learn how to research."

- "We have found that just letting the professor know that we are here and have the resources to help is usually enough. I have told new members of the faculty or the faculty in my liaison departments some of the resources we have added recently and invite them over to see what we have. I have invited some to tour areas of the library, especially those in which they have interest. Almost all like a tour of our archives and special collections. I emphasize items from the collections which might be useful in presentations. I have yet to meet a 'defensive' faculty member here."

Offering to assist can be straightforward, such as a simple expression of availability. Telling an instructor that particular class assignments are outdated, poorly worded, or otherwise difficult for students to complete requires a different type of interaction, one that involves less-than-positive feedback and usually implies some kind of criticism. The necessity of these types of interactions underlies the importance of developing trust-based relationships with faculty.

Librarians suggested several ways to improve assignments, including:

• "I would never correct the professor's wording, either privately or publicly, to him or one of his students. When a student asks what a professor means by a phrase, we either look it up or I ask the student's perception—as the student has had more experience with the professor than I have. If the problem is beyond both of us, I encourage the student to e-mail the professor directly. I offer the student use of my e-mail with the understanding that I will relay any answer back to the student."

• "That can be tricky, but, again, be direct. Point out the library changed things and they do keep changing, and offer to update the class. In terms of poorly worded assignments, calling for clarification can be tricky. If the students are really stuck, it's best to make the call."

• "'We've noticed at the reference desk that your students are having trouble interpreting your assignment. So that we can be sure that we're pointing the students in the right direction in the library, I was hoping that you and I could meet to go over the assignment and, perhaps, clarify some of the wording' or 'We've noticed at the reference desk that your students are having trouble interpreting your assignment. I hope you don't mind but I've taken the liberty of reading through the assignment sheet and have made some suggestions for changes that might help students understand the assignment within the context of our library.'"

• "This is generally where I try to do an intervention of some sort. Again, using e-mail as the point of contact (unless it is critical to call due to timing or to intense demand being placed on the library by poorly informed students), I indicate that professor X's class is currently using the library to work on a particular assignment but that there seems to be some difficulty in understanding how to best use library resources. I then offer to provide an orientation, and since this is generally at the time when everyone is feverishly trying to finish the assignment, I also offer to provide small group sessions for the students if that would be more convenient. While time-consuming, even small group sessions would be preferable to the one-on-one instruction for the same questions that are being provided through the reference staff. I also offer to provide an orientation for future semesters when this class is offered, hoping to get a foot in the door and do some 'preventative' instruction.

Which method you elect to employ depends greatly on your own personality and your relationship with the faculty member involved.

ADVICE FROM LIBRARIANS AND FACULTY

The last survey question asked of librarians and faculty inquired about advice that they would have for librarians new to collaboration. Following is a selection of responses to that question.

From faculty:

- "Let us know you are willing to do this [collaborate]."
- "Approach as a scholarly/professional endeavor, geared to faculty's expressed needs, their course structures, academic requirements, and constraints, and do not assume they know how much you know. Build good bridges and know your audience."
- "Be bold, be bold, but not too bold. Patience is a good concept. A gently asserted patient assertion of your own reality is often very instructive. When we share enthusiasm and growth, we build respect and a better academic community. Respect for students and concern to help them and to learn from them is something librarians and teachers can and ought to share. Also, a professionally usable exchange of appreciative and praising memos is a good way to solidify teacher–librarian collaboration: we're all going for promotion sometime, so a file full of expressed appreciation and positive evaluation can help both sides if sides there are."
- "Good communication is essential if librarians are to provide course-related instruction. Therefore, faculty should meet with librarians formally and informally throughout the semester. Faculty and librarians should collaboratively develop an active program of instruction with sessions in and out of the classroom timed to coincide with assignments which require use of library resources."

- "Librarians are the experts in a very fast-changing information environment, and faculty rely on them to provide updated access and advice to obtaining information. We have a hard time keeping up with our areas of research, our classes, and our (unfortunate) committee work—therefore, make it easy, accessible, and understandable. Demonstrate the advantages of new systems/databases. Uncover [reveal] was introduced here recently, and [the librarians] did a very good job of introducing the system to faculty and making it easy and accessible in a training session where we identified what journals we wanted on our index. This was great, and I'm grateful for the service. They are also personable, interested in good work, and have non-antagonistic attitudes toward the faculty. This all helps."

- "Be sensitive to people's professional/time schedules. Some faculty may be easier to work with than others."

- "Let the faculty member know your areas of interest and your background. Keep the faculty informed of acquisitions and new services related to teaching and scholarship. Be a scholar yourself."

- "Tell them about the type of collaboration that you are interested in doing and see if anyone is willing to try it. It's great to talk face to face with people. If you have a faculty lunch room, try eating with new people. Most faculty are great at networking."

- "Know a faculty's needs and [that] everyone is different. Only when a librarian knows each faculty's individual needs can this kind of collaboration be worked out."

- "Many times, new instructors or part-time instructors simply don't know that the librarian(s) is willing and able to do…and that they *want* to be involved! I guess it's a matter of getting to know one another, often not an easy task."

From Librarians:

- "You are the librarian, a trained professional. You are a valuable resource, but you are not the course teacher. The class is under the teacher's control. Never get between a student and teacher."

- "Be secure that your skills are unique and a wonderful complement to their knowledge. Let them know that you know they have specialized knowledge, and that you would like to team with them whenever possible to take advantage of the synergy you can create together. Your knowledge of the rapidly changing library/ information world together with their knowledge of the subject area!"

- "Take the same stance with advanced graduate students, too. Let them know you respect that all the work they have put into their studies is creating an expertise such that although they come to you for consultation about their research, you depend on them to work *with* you in order to approach their research project with the best key terms, background understanding, etc. Model collaboration with these folks (they'll be faculty later, quite likely, and will look to librarians for collaboration if you model it for them now!)."

- One librarian recommended that you:
  1. "Know your field (journals, articles, ref tools, books, Web, etc.)
  2. Be forward, not aggressive—offer services, be flexible in dates and times
  3. *Never* assume anything—but do not insult or act inappropriate if, say, a faculty/adjunct does not know what ERIC is.
  4. Be open to new ideas and methods
  5. Make sure you really *want* to do what's proposed!"

- "In general, work with those people who are interested in what you have to offer. Don't worry about the holdouts. In working with faculty, if you expect them to be open to your suggestions for changes and improvements in their class assignments, be sure that you are open to suggestions for changes and improvements in the way you provide instruction/reference services."

- "I have found it useful to build a strong relationship with a small group of faculty members to begin with and then use their recommendations to make contact with other faculty members. In other words, start out small, build trust and respect within that small circle, and then let your circle of influence grow. Oh, and don't get discouraged—it took me over a year to build collaborative relationships when I first came to campus."

• "Respect their time; keep things short, direct, to the point. Do your homework; have something of value to offer. Don't expect everything to work with everyone. Keep trying. Learn what you can about department politics and problems so you don't leap into difficult areas unawares."

• "Keep trying!"

• "Be diplomatic in your collaboration with them. Offer suggestions or options and let them decide what they want in terms of instruction. Do not try to tell them what to do."

• "To be friendly, helpful, and persistent. I really believe that if you make an effort to discover the interests of the faculty first, your efforts to collaborate will be more fruitful."

• "General advice: talk the talk. What are the teaching faculty interested in? tenure and promotion? We as librarians also have some of the same requirements. Therefore, I try to casually bring up my research when talking with faculty. I also use my research for examples in BI sessions, especially graduate level. Things like the time constraints I have in doing research, dealing with journals that change publisher or editor, slow response time from editors, glitches in research or writing, subject research that I have done that will help them."

• "I would advise that person to be as forthright and forceful as possible. If you truly believe that library instruction is useful, you can find a way to convey that to faculty. On the other hand, if you don't care if the students learn anything, that will also be conveyed. A genuine concern for students' learning experiences will provide an excellent model on which to base your actions."

• "I cannot emphasize enough the importance of personal contact, and building a rapport. There is simply no substitute for the personal relationships you develop over time. Any opportunity to develop such contacts should be explored. Attending departmental functions, e-mailing faculty about interesting books in their areas, responding promptly to requests for information.

While these are not BI activities, the increased exposure can generate BI requests."

• "Don't agree to do something that you know from experience doesn't work well just because the faculty person asks for it."

• "Clear communication with concrete suggestions of how the librarian can help, framed in a pleasant, collegial tone is the best way to deal with the teaching faculty. As always, treating others as we want to be treated professionally is the best mechanism for good working relationships."

• "Get out there and walk the halls."

CONCLUSIONS

The responses to this survey, despite its small sample, do provide some suggestions concerning how librarians can approach the responsibilities of librarian–faculty collaboration and how to facilitate and develop collaborative relationships. Most ideas are quite practical and reflect common sense. If librarians practice these suggestions, eventually they can build relationships with faculty that extend beyond the collection development or the single library instruction session.

To be an effective collaborator, you must learn to think of yourself as a networker, creating partnerships across your campus. When you communicate with faculty by attending departmental meetings, increasing personal contact, and building a rapport, you will be networking within your institution—all efforts that will lead to opportunities for sustained collaboration. As you grow more adept and develop positive relationships, your networking opportunities will increase. You as a librarian will help shape the evolution of educational institutions.

A Postmodern Directory of Electronic Resources on Librarians and Faculty Working Together

Dane Ward
Central Michigan University

Doug Cook
Shippensburg University

As we speed into the twenty-first century on the coattails of technology and globalization, we find ourselves awash in a sea of transient information. This is especially true in the dynamic electronic environment where Web pages surface briefly and disappear. We can no longer expect the constancy of information and its retrieval that we did in the past. The creation of information has taken on a life of its own, and users have developed a wide variety of frequently idiosyncratic search strategies. In response to this changing universe, those of us concerned with providing access to relevant information must explore alternative models for organizing resources and teaching research. In the area of library-based instruction, many practitioners have moved away from teaching linear research processes and replaced them with more nonlinear, dynamic models.

We live in what some have called the postmodern era. Traditional hierarchical boundaries have blurred, and emergent structures of organization are characterized by fluidity and flow. The only constant is change, and we each construct—from the pieces available to us—unique ways of working, playing, and being. The notion of static bibliographies or directories in this environment seems increasingly obsolete. By the time of publication, many of the cited print sources are out-of-date and many of the Web sites are no longer available.

A postmodern directory, if such a thing could even exist, must still provide users with guidance in finding information on a given topic. However, in articulation, this variation on an old research tool is no longer simply a list of Web sites divided into convenient categories. It must be a creative, multifaceted project. The postmodern directory provides access to resources through various means. In this way, it lessens the effects of rapid change, the obsolescence of Web sites, and the variety of learning styles.

Paradoxically, this directory resembles a well-organized collage with its pieces overlapping into related categories and categories themselves blending into each other. The content of this directory looks very much like a "traditional" directory of Web sites, electronic discussions, and online journals. However, in contrast to these other sources of information, it also incorporates more enduring access points and tools, such as "engines" or services that search specifically for electronic discussions and e-journals. In addition, it includes a long list of concepts and phrases that might be used to search the Web for sites concerning collaboration on campus or with librarians.

With this directory, we hope to provide useful information about librarian–faculty collaboration, while striving to place this issue in a broader discussion of campus collaboration. Efforts to facilitate working relationships between librarians and faculty are paralleled by others on campus, such as those between student and academic services. Ultimately, we attempt to provide access to specific Web sites, as well as to broader formulations and models wherever they exist. One might see such a directory as a Rorschach test of its creators' interests and proclivities in specific areas of collaboration.

CONCEPTS RELEVANT TO LIBRARIAN–FACULTY COLLABORATION

Finding Web-based information about librarian–faculty collaboration can be complicated for a number of reasons. For one, the terminology is constantly evolving. *Collaboration* is a newer term that has been more popular in the 1990s, whereas the term *partnerships* was more common in the 1980s. The problem of language becomes further confused when authors talk loosely about *collaboration* as a synonym for other terms. Most often, *collaboration* is used interchangeably with the terms *cooperation* and *coordination*, though these refer to less interdependent, integrated relationships.

Another difficulty has to do with our grasp of the broader terms used in higher education to refer to working relationships that incorporate librarian–faculty collaboration. For instance, learning communities, which integrate the contents of several courses into a more seamless learning experience for students, involve a great deal of collaboration between instructors. Librarians are often important participants in learning communities.

Participation in the interdisciplinary dialogue occurring on our campuses requires that we remain alert to the evolving language of working together. Figure 1 lists some terms that will continue to be useful in finding Web sites on collaboration.

Figure 1. Search Terms for Finding Web Sites on Collaboration.

General Terms

Bridge building	Interaction
Coalition	Networking
Collusion	Participation
Connection	Partnership
Cooperation	Relationship
Coordination	Team

Figure 1 *cont*. Search Terms for Finding Web Sites on Collaboration.

Library-Related Terms
College and university libraries, relations
with faculty and curriculum
Evidence-based medicine and librarians
Faculty and librarian partnerships
Faculty and librarians as colleagues
Faculty–librarian interaction
Information literacy and faculty
Librarian–faculty relations
Librarian–teacher cooperation
Librarians–college staff relations
Resource-based learning and librarians

Broader Terms Related to Education in General
Collaborative learning
College personnel and collaboration
Coordinated studies programs
Course clusters
Digital libraries
Education and partnership
Education and collaboration
Federated learning communities
Freshman interest groups
Learning communities
Learning organizations
Learning partnerships
Linked courses
Student affairs and collaboration
Student personnel and collaboration
Student services and collaboration
Team teaching
Work teams

WEB SITES ON COLLABORATION

In our effort to provide structure to a marvelously chaotic universe of Web sites, the authors of this essay have divided the following list into several broad categories. The authors begin by exploring formal programs of librarian–faculty collaboration, being careful to make a distinction between those based primarily on technology and those that are not. This is followed by a brief list of Web-based articles. The authors then offer several groupings of sites from various professions, organizations, and coalitions within higher education that have pursued similar initiatives. These are designated as "Campuswide Discussions of Collaboration," "Collaboration Beyond Campus," "Organizations with an Interest in Librarian–Faculty Collaboration," and "Other Organizations interested in Campus Collaboration." The essay ends with a section on finding online journals about collaboration.

This directory provides a list of Web sites that were available at the time of publication. Inevitably, some of them will no longer be accessible when you begin to research this list. As a strategy, the authors recommend that you use the terms and topics provided in the previous section of this essay to help find more current sites.

INSTRUCTIONAL COLLABORATIONS BASED ON TECHNOLOGY

The Collaboratory (http://library.lib.binghamton.edu/subjects/polsci/collab.html). This site describes Binghamton University Library's program to enhance the teaching of library and information skills with technology. Samples of courses are included.

Librarian–Faculty Teaching Technology Partnerships (http://www.library.arizona.edu/partnerships/welcome.html). From the University of Arizona Library, this collection provides an extensive list of courses in which librarians and faculty are collaborating to integrate technology into the curriculum. Each course description includes collaborators' names, project summary, assignments, and related Web sites.

Partnerships for Learning (http://ublib.buffalo.edu/libraries/ projects/learning/learn2.html). This site from the University of Buffalo lists collaborative campus activities, including great models of faculty and librarians working together to develop course Web sites. See especially the links entitled "The World Wide Web in the Classroom" and "Collaborating to Create Digital Collections."

TWIST: Teaching with Innovative Style and Technology (http:// twist.lib.uiowa. edu/index.html). Created at the University of Iowa, TWIST is a project designed as a "model training program for librarians and faculty on networked information resources." The project includes designing and evaluating Web-based tutorials, formal pairing of instructional faculty and librarians; plus courses with Web sites collaboratively produced by these faculty–librarian teams. The site lists these collaborative teams and the sites they have created. A well-developed poster session of one such effort can be found at http://twist.lib.uiowa.edu/about/acrl.pdf.

The UWired Project: Building an Electronic Community (http:/ /www.washington.edu/uwired). This well-known project at the University of Washington involves collaborations among groups on campus to integrate electronic communication and information skills into the teaching process. Their pages include descriptions of topics such as the UWired collaboratories and commons, freshman interest groups, the interdisciplinary writing program, and both internal and external collaborations.

INSTRUCTIONAL COLLABORATIONS NOT DEPENDING PRIMARILY ON TECHNOLOGY

Collaborating for Information Literacy in Graduate Education via the World Wide Web (http://www.tiac.net/users/ludcke/keh/ collab.html). This site represents the efforts of a Lesley College librarian and faculty member to facilitate development of information literacy among graduate education students. It describes a project emphasizing the case study method, as well as cooperative learning activities.

How to Build Librarian/Instructional Faculty Collaborative Partnerships (http://www2.hawaii.edu/~kroddy/poster/). This page summarizes the experiences of four institutions and provides a list of ideas called "How to Form Collaborative Partnerships with Instructional Faculty." Originally a poster session sponsored by the ACRL Instruction Section's Teaching Methods Committee at the 1997 ALA Annual Conference, it includes "Team Teaching with Instructional Faculty," "Creating General Education Curriculum with Instructional Faculty," "Oberlin's Faculty Information Literacy Workshop," and "Helping UW Athletes Get Wired."

Instructional Teams at Indiana University-Purdue University Indianapolis (http://www-lib.iupui.edu/itt/). This page describes a major collaborative effort at IUPUI that teams individual faculty members, librarians, technologists, counselors, and student mentors to prepare or revise courses. It links to other interesting local pages, including "Collaborating with Librarians on Instructional Teams," "Resources" (with an essay by Philip Tompkins called *The Reality of Instructional Teams),* "Team Products," and "University Library Instructional Teams."

The Learning Community at Wayne State University (http://www.langlab.wayne.edu/TLC/TLChome.html). This summary describes an experimental program designed for "at-risk" freshmen. Students enroll in an integrated block of courses in English, speech, computer literacy, reading and study skills, and the university orientation/information literacy course. The program involves collaboration among faculty, librarians, and student services staff, who meet on a weekly basis.

Project Renaissance (http://www.albany.edu/projren/9697/hutech/projren.html). This project from the University of Albany is similar to Wayne State's Learning Community but is much larger in scope. Based on teams of one hundred students, it creates a unified year-long living/learning experience focusing on the themes of technology and human identity. Participants include full-time and part-time faculty, librarians, student services staff, as well as upper-division mentors.

ARTICLES ON LIBRARIAN AND FACULTY COLLABORATION
Collaboration: Partnerships between Librarians and Information Technologists (http://www.ukoln.ac.uk/services/papers/bl/rdr6250/lippincott.html). Based on a 1996 presentation given by Joan Lippincott at a United Kingdom conference on "Networked Information in an International Context," this paper gives definitions of collaboration and examples of partnerships between librarians and IT professionals. It also looks at factors that promote and inhibit collaborative projects.

Faculty–Librarian Collaboration in Building the Curriculum for the Millenium—the US Experience (http://ifla.inist.fr/IV/ifla64/040-112e.htm). Written by Hannelore Rader and presented at the 64th IFLA Conference in 1998, this paper explores trends in librarian and faculty collaboration in higher education. Focusing primarily on information literacy, she provides summaries from a number of schools.

Librarian and Faculty Partnerships for Distance Education (http://wings.buffalo.edu/publications/mcjrnl/v4n1/platt.html). Written by Holly Heller-Ross for *MC Journal: The Journal of Academic Media Librarianship* (summer 1996), this article describes collaborative efforts of librarians and faculty in the Telenursing Distance Education Program at the State University of New York at Plattsburgh.

Navigating the Universe of Web Information in the Multimedia Classroom (http://www.library.ucsb.edu/universe/edwards.html). Doralyn Edwards discusses the management of collaborative efforts from the perspective of a librarian working with electronic information sources, creating Web pages, and teaching the Internet. The author discusses how this changes the role of librarians.

Redefining Roles: Librarians as Partners in Information Literacy Education (http://netways.shef.ac.uk/rbase/papers/zaldwill.htm). Helene Williams and Anne Zald describe the collaborative role of librarians at the University of Washington in transforming the undergraduate curriculum, facilities, and teaching practices. It focuses primarily on developing an information literacy program.

Shared Vision: Learning Partnerships for the Information Age (http://www.ualberta.ca/dept/slis/cais/laverty.htm). This article by Corinne Laverty and Martin Schiralli describes collaborative instructional efforts at Queen's University to teach computer and information skills.

CAMPUSWIDE DISCUSSIONS OF COLLABORATION: LEARNING COMMUNITIES

Integrating Library Instruction into Learning Communities: A L.E.A.P. toward Innovation (http://www.libraries.psu.edu/crsweb/docs/future2/sld001.htm). In a useful PowerPoint presentation, authors Debora Cheney and Helen M. Sheehy, from the Social Sciences Library at Penn State, focus on practical aspects of integrating the library into larger learning communities.

Learning Communities: Building Gateways to Student Success (http://soeweb.syr. edu/hed/tinto/acpa.htm). This valuable essay by learning community advocate Vincent Tinto of Syracuse University also provides a bibliography on collaborative learning and a list of relevant electronic discussions and Web sites.

Maricopa Community College: Integrated Learning Garden (http://www.mcli.dist.maricopa.edu/ilc/index.html). This marvelous page describes the essential components of learning communities, as well as five working models. Other sections consist of stories from students, frequently asked questions, and reports from other institutions.

USF Learning Communities (http://www.usf.edu/~lc/). This University of South Florida site provides a great deal of information about that institution's learning community initiatives that began with a grant from the Fund for Improvement in Post Secondary Education (FIPSE). It provides a large hyperlinked list of institutions supporting learning communities. Of special interest is the effort to incorporate information literacy into a MOO-based course and in writing across the curriculum.

COLLABORATION BEYOND CAMPUS

Center for the Study of Work Teams (http://www.workteams. unt.edu/index.htm). Based at the University of North Texas, this center focuses on education and research in all areas of teaming. The site includes links to conference proceedings, articles, research projects, opportunities for participation, and links to related works.

Collaboration Framework—Addressing Community Capacity (http://www. cyfernet.org/nnco/framework.html). Created by the National Network for Collaboration, this effort is aimed at groups that wish to start or strengthen collaborative community projects. Information is included about initiating collaborations and defining collaborator roles.

DLib Edu: Collaboratory for Digital Libraries Education (http://www.scils.rutgers.edu/lis/digitalsplash.html). DLib Edu is intended as a central site for information on the development of digital libraries.

Model Organizational Structures and Best Practices or Successful National Collaborative Information Partnerships (http://www.ed.gov/pubs/Structures/index.html).This is Patricia Libutti's 1997 document discussing the development of networks and collaborations in the context of providing education information.

ORGANIZATIONS WITH AN INTEREST IN LIBRARIAN/FACULTY COLLABORATION

Association of College and Research Libraries (http://www.ala.org/acrl). This professional organization of academic librarians supports a site that includes papers from the 1997 and 1999 ACRL National Conferences. Several papers at these sites highlight the collaboration of librarians with other parts of the campus community:

1997 ACRL Conference Papers (http://www.ala.org/acrl/papers.html#Partners)

1. Partnerships and Competition by Kate Nevins. In this keynote address, Nevins talks about the reasons that libraries have succeeded with collaborative initiatives, as well as the challenges of partnering with nonlibrary organizations and the benefits of partnering.

2. Expanding the Role of the Library in Teaching and Learning: Distance Learning Initiatives by Carolyn A. Snyder, Susan Logue and Barbara G. Preece. The authors focus primarily on academic library involvement in distance learning programs and, specifically, the administrative issues. However, the authors also discuss the importance of collaboration between on- and off-campus partners.

3. Collaborating with Faculty in Preparing Students for the Asynchronous Classro om by Kay E. Harvey and Nancy H. Dewald. Librarians play a leadership role by partnering with faculty and technical support personnel to prepare students for the new educational paradigms of active and collaborative learning in an asynchronous environment. Penn State's Project Vision is used as a model.

1999 ACRL Conference Papers (http://www.ala.org/acrl/pdfpapers99.html).

1. A Successful Partnership Library by Nick Lund and Pamela M. Blome. In this article, the authors discuss a successful library partnership between Northern Arizona University in Yuma and Arizona Western College on their shared campus in southwest Arizona's Yuma County.

2. *Common Ground: Creating a Unified Environmental Information System through Stakeholder Partnership* by Linda Langschied. There are numerous benefits of partnerships between librarians, government officials, scientists, and the public to improve access to environmental information.

3. *First-Year Learning Communities: Redefining the Educational Roles of Academic Librarians* by Tony Stamatoplos and Terry Taylor. The authors discuss collaboration between faculty and professional staff at Indiana University/Purdue University at Indianapolis (IUPUI) and DePaul University to create an integrated curriculum for all first-year students.

4. *Learning Communities, Adult Learners, and Instructional Teams at IUPUI* by May Jafari. This paper discusses the Adult Learning Community at IUPUI. The unique needs of the adult learner and the challenges of collaborating with faculty are explored.

American Association for Higher Education (AAHE) (http://www.aahe.org). Concerned with a variety of higher education issues, this site includes links to "Program for the Promotion of Institutional Change" and "Powerful Partnerships: A Shared Responsibility for Learning," a joint report of AAHE, the American College Personnel Association, and the National Association of Student Personnel Administrators. In addition, the Teaching, Learning & Technology Roundtable (http://www.tltgroup.org/programs/round.html) program focuses on creating campus teams (including librarians) to improve teaching in higher education.

American Educational Research Association (AERA) (http://www.aera.net/). This organization, which includes a special interest group on information technology and library resources, represents another opportunity for collaboration.

Association of Research Libraries (ARL) (http://www.arl.org/arl/proceedings/index.html). The proceedings of membership meetings offer a variety of papers, some related to collaboration. See for

instance "The Partnership between Scholars and Librarians" by
Phyllis Franklin in the 1996 proceedings.

EDUCAUSE (http://www.educause.edu/). Educause's mission is
"to be an indispensable partner in enabling the transformational
changes occurring in higher education through the effective
management and use of information resources—technology,
services, and information." See particularly Educause's publications
Cause/Effect and *Educom Review.* Educause's Library/IT
Partnership Constituency Group (http://www.educause.edu/
memdir/cg/libit.html) includes an electronic discussion and
proceedings of the 1996 conference.

Coalition for Networked Information (http://www.cni.org/). This
organization seeks to promote partnerships in higher education
among professionals working with networked information. See
especially "Creating New Learning Communities via the Network"
(http://www.cni.org/projects/nlc/). On this page, you can find the
1996 keynote presentation at the ALA's preconference on "Librarian
Leaders in New Learning Communities," by Roberta S. Matthews.
CNI's pages are well worth the exploration, as they are full of
interesting collaborations.

OTHER ORGANIZATIONS CONCERNED WITH CAMPUS COLLABORATION

Association of American Colleges and Universities (http://
www.aacu-edu.org/home.html). This Web site includes much
information about collaborative initiatives. One priority area is
"Mobilizing Collaborative Leadership for Educational and
Institutional Effectiveness." The group also sponsors a Collaborative
Leadership Institute. Interestingly, librarians seem absent from these
discussions.

ERIC Clearinghouse on Higher Education (http://
www.eriche.org). This great site located at George Washington
University provides access to the clearinghouse's newsletter, digests

(summaries of important issues), subject bibliographies, book reviews and descriptions of educational trends. Although not specifically concerned with librarian–faculty collaboration, it does provide information about other efforts, including between student and academic services.

League for Innovation in the Community College (http://www.league.org). The league is a "non-profit educational consortium of leading community colleges," working for innovation in that educational context. The Web site includes current and back issues of their publications *Leadership Abstracts* and *Learning Abstracts*, which contain articles of relevance. For instance, the October 1999 issue of *Leadership Abstracts* contains an article on collaborative change by Steven W. Gilbert called "Preserve and Transform: Integrating Technology into Academic Life."

NASPA, Student Affairs Administrators in Higher Education (http://www.naspa.org/). Student affairs has a long history of working toward collaboration with the instructional faculty on our campuses. Some years ago, former ACRL president Patricia Senn Breivik told one of the authors that librarians would be well advised to look at their efforts. *NASPA Online* provides links to a variety of student affairs–related topics, as well as a page that gives members an opportunity to highlight collaborative work with teaching faculty.

ONLINE JOURNALS CONCERNED WITH CAMPUS COLLABORATION
There are thousands of online journals on the Web, free to anyone who can find them. Online catalogs can help. Included below are first, two "catalogs" of online journals, and second, a list of journals that contain articles relevant to the authors' interest in librarians and classroom faculty working together.

TOOLS FOR FINDING ONLINE JOURNALS
BUBL Journals (http://bubl.ac.uk/journals/). From the BUBL Information Service, a United Kingdom program from Strathclyde University in Scotland, this site provides a list of more than two

hundred online journals in various subject categories. Some of these provide full-text articles, though most deliver only abstracts.

Scholarly Journals Distributed via the World Wide Web (http://info.lib.uh.edu/wj/alpha.html). This site from the University of Houston Libraries provides a fine alphabetical list of electronic journals by title. Journals of possible interest include *Educational Technology and Society* and *International Electronic Journal for Leadership in Learning,* and *The Katherine Sharp Review*

Online Journals Relevant to Librarian and Faculty Collaboration
Cause/Effect (http://www.educause.edu/pub/ce/cause-effect.html). Subtitled "a practitioner's journal about managing and using information resources on college and university campuses," it represents a forum for articles on collaboration. See the spring 1997 article, "The Electronic Library: New Roles for Librarians," by Brendan A. Rapple, with commentaries by Joanne R. Euster, Susan Perry, and Jim Schmidt.

College Quarterly (http://www.senecac.on.ca/quarterly/index.html). This "journal of professional development for college educators" includes articles such as "Library Assignments: A Teacher–Librarian Partnership" by Rhonda Roth in the winter 1993 issue. Articles are searchable by date, author, or subject.

DeLiberations on Teaching and Learning in Higher Education (http://www.lgu.ac.uk/deliberations/home.html). This is the outcome of "the Interactive Electronic Magazine Project" at London Guildhall University. Designed to be a "a resource for educational developers, librarians, academic staff and managers in education," it provides articles, Web sites, and information arranged by subject discipline and topic.

Educom Review (http://www.educause.edu/pub/er/erm.html). *Educom Review* "explores the changing ways we will work, learn, and communicate in the digital world of the 21st century." Though focusing on communications technology, collaborative issues are often discussed, particularly as they relate to technology.

Interactions (http://www.warwick.ac.uk/ETS/interactions/). Published by the Educational Technology Service at the University of Warwick (United Kingdom), this electronic journal (aimed at that institution's faculty and staff) targets the improvement of teaching and learning with technology.

MC Journal: The Journal of Academic Media Librarianship (http://wings. buffalo.edu/publications/mcjrnl/). This journal focuses on issues related to audiovisual librarianship, including "a/v production, collection development, cataloging, storage and preservation of materials, media center management, copyright, and emerging technologies." One collaborative article from this journal is Holly Heller-Ross's "Librarian and Faculty Partnerships for Distance Education."

National Teaching & Learning Forum (http://www.ntlf.com/). This outstanding subscription publication (permitting free access to five recent issues) concerns all aspects of teaching in higher education and represents a potential venue for discussions on the development of librarian–faculty collaboration.

THE Journal (http://www.thejournal.com/). This journal focuses primarily on the use of technology and its integration into the curriculum. Many collaborative efforts and opportunities are highlighted.

Strategies for Finding Relevant Electronic Discussions

Finally, the diligent researcher will find numerous catalogs and search engines that provide access to electronic discussions and educational chats on various topics. Currently, few discussions exist specifically on the topic of librarian–faculty collaboration, but possibilities within discussions devoted to the subject disciplines represent tremendous opportunities. The issue of collaboration appears in discussions in other contexts as well, including those focusing on elementary and secondary education, business, industry, and government. Again, the authors would recommend experimenting with the terms and phrases identified at the beginning of this postmodern directory.

GUIDES AND CATALOGS OF ONLINE DISCUSSIONS

Forum One (http://www.ForumOne.com/). This guide claims to provide access to more than 310,000 online discussions.

L-Soft International (http://www.lsoft.com/lists/list_q.html). This search engine comes from the company that produces the listserv software.

List of Lists (http://catalog.com/vivian/interest-group-search.html).

Liszt, the Mailing List Directory (http://www.liszt.com/). This site includes more than 90,000 lists.

N2H2 Directory of Scholarly and Professional E-Conferences (http://n2h2.com/KOVACS/.

TILE.NET (http://www.tile.net/).

Library-Oriented Lists and Electronic Serials (http://www.wrlc.org/liblists/).

New-List (http://scout.cs.wisc.edu/caservices/new-list/index.html). From the Internet Scout Project at the University of Wisconsin, this site identifies new lists and archives older ones.

CONCLUSION

The Internet has become the great collaborative tool of the Information Age. Individuals and groups create their Web sites, offering observations, research, and expertise to an increasingly interconnected world, which takes bits and pieces of this and that to construct its own meanings.

Naturally, a postmodern directory has no end. At best, it serves as a pointer to the universe of realities and possibilities. Hopefully, you have found sites that currently exist, as well as those that exist in the "parallel" universes of education, industry, business, and government. Ultimately, the authors hope that by providing access to a variety of far-ranging resources, this directory will contribute in some small way to the creation of other collaborative realities.

The Future of Collaboration between Librarians and Teaching Faculty

Jean Caspers
Oregon State University

Katy Lenn
University of Oregon

Predicting the future is risky business in any situation, but it is magnified when looking at higher education. The fundamental challenge of the librarian will be to deal with the turbulence wrought by change, change in information technology, in the profession, and in higher education. Changes in higher education, in particular, may drastically affect the idea and practice of collaboration with faculty. Pressures to economize are resulting in major cost-cutting initiatives on most campuses at the same time new technologies are changing the way people work and study. As faculty contend with an educational system in flux, these environmental pushes and pulls can help and hinder librarian–faculty collaboration.

148

COST-CUTTING

Unfortunately, the cost-cutting trend of increasing reliance on adjunct faculty greatly impacts collaboration. The norm will no longer be collaboration based on years of contacts and interactions. Librarians will need to make an extra effort in working with adjunct faculty who teach on an irregular basis and do not spend a good deal of time on campus. This may involve working up a collaborative project without the faculty member and then presenting it as a semideveloped idea.

Faculty face increasing demands for more time in the classroom and yet also are dealing with decreases in research funding. The key to establishing a good collaborative effort is to deliver a proposal that is not only pedagogically sound but also addresses or assists the faculty members as they deal with the pressures of economy.

TECHNOLOGY

Technology has been a constant theme throughout this book. It has served as a catalyst for many collaborative ideas. Librarians are viewed by many instructional faculty as technical "experts." As technology evolves, however, faculty may feel that librarian interaction is not essential because students are perceived as being more computer/Internet savvy.

Peter F. Drucker has suggested that we can understand the power of technology by considering modern parallels to changes affected by the invention of the printing press and movable type between 1450 and 1455.[1] Drucker pointed out that in the fifteenth century, printing technologists were initially catapulted into the wealthy and elite of society; however, over time their authority and preeminence did not last. The more lasting legacy came during the next century. Those innovators with their focus on technology became craftsmen, valued, but not an elite. It was those who dealt with the content of publications who became the more influential and powerful citizens.

Similarly, as information technologies become more fully integrated into the everyday life of students and scholars, the librarian's expertise as a technologist will take a back seat to his or her role as an information professional. Academic librarians with expertise in organizing and retrieving content, and with teaching-related skills and concepts will have much to offer to faculty. In order to reach students, librarians today, more than in the past, must promote collaboration as a value-added prospect.

Sheila D. Creth addressed this issue, listing the core values of the library profession as "service, quality, universal access, and cooperation." She indicated that the library's role during the current era of fast change should be ". . . characterized by visibility and vitality . . . . This means that academic librarians should be valued as essential to the teaching, learning and research activities of the university. Librarians, not solely the collections or the library building, should be valued and considered an integral member (sic) of the university teaching and research team."[2]

Technology can create challenges to building relationships with faculty. The use of voice mail and e-mail reduces the amount of face-to-face contact with faculty, making it potentially harder to establish the kind of collegial relationship enjoyed by the editors of this book—Dick Raspa and Dane Ward. Effort should be made to supplement electronic communication outreach to faculty in their offices and meetings over coffee.

Distance education also presents a host of unique collaboration opportunities and challenges. Because students in distance-delivered courses are not likely to walk into the library building on campus, their institution's library may be invisible to them. Unless librarians market their resources and services, these students may complete their programs without benefit of the library. Faculty who use libraries in person may not conceive of how students in distance-delivered programs can use their institution's library. The most effective way for librarians to reach distance learners is not through publications distributed to students or Web pages linked from the library's home page promoting library services for distance learners; rather, it is through cooperation (at least) and collaboration (at best) with teaching faculty. Because faculty are the conduit to distance education students, communicating with them about their students' research needs and providing realistic responses to those needs is critical.

PROMOTING THE COLLABORATIVE ROLE OF LIBRARIANS IN TEACHING AND LEARNING

Previous essays in this book have identified numerous examples of librarians and teaching faculty working together. Two types of collaborations have been highlighted.

Examples of individual librarian–teaching faculty collaborations have been described in the essay, "Case Studies in Collaboration." This type of collaborating is often experienced as exciting because it is so unique. Because few librarians are working collaboratively with teaching faculty, the opportunity to do so seems unusual. How do we create a climate where the contributions of librarians to teaching and learning are recognized, expected, and valued by the teaching faculty across the academy?

The answer is always the same: by seeking collaborative opportunities with faculty all the time. The news of successful collaboration will spread among the faculty in contact with the collaborators. If the collaborators go on to speak at conferences, particularly at nonlibrary conferences as Raspa and Ward have done, their efforts will potentially have a ripple effect at other institutions.

Moreover, complementary top-down efforts also must be made. In her essay "Building Coalitions for Information Literacy," Abigal Loomis asserted that to make library instruction visible on campus, a range of coalitions must be built.[3] To do this, we librarians must define our place as teachers in the educational mission of our institutions. We must answer the question, how do we function as teachers in higher education? We begin this process by building coalitions within the library itself in support of the teaching role of librarians.

After the internal commitment to the teaching role of librarians is established, we need to market our instructional role to the campus. This requires political skills, including ". . . negotiation, persuasion, compromise and strategizing in order to achieve certain objectives."[4] At the levels where curriculum is determined, the case for information literacy needs to be made. Deans and department heads must be convinced of three things: that students must learn how to access and use information; that these skills should be integrated across the disciplines; and that librarians working collaboratively with faculty are the appropriate instructional team to achieve this goal.

LIBRARIANS AS RESEARCH COLLABORATORS

In his address to the ARL Membership Meeting program on redefining higher education, Stanley Chodorow spoke as both medieval scholar and the provost of the University of Pennsylvania. Like Drucker, Chodorow reflected on the Middle Ages. "In the not-so-distant future," he stated, "our own intellectual culture will begin to look something like the medieval one. Our scholarly and information environment will have territories dominated by the content, rather than by distinct individual contributions."[5] His view of the future suggests that scholars will work together on common projects, rather than individually producing scholarly works upon which others will build. The fluidity and rapidity of scholarly exchange on the Internet and the nature of the electronic publication will give birth to the era of collaborative enterprise. Electronically shared documents, he predicted, may become like those of the medieval works that ". . . flowed from author to author, across generations, growing and changing as individual contributors worked on them."[6]

Chodorow suggested that a primary role for librarians will be that of cataloging and organizing information on the Internet for the benefit of scholars and students who need to find it. He shared with his audience of librarians how copyright practice and the concept of autonomous authorship will change to accommodate electronic modes of scholarly discourse and publishing. Management of information author by author will no longer suffice.

Although Chodorow focused on the role of the librarian in service to the scholars as the organizer of information, he referred to Umberto Eco's ideal of the medieval librarian,

> the information scholar who held the key to knowing. The librarian of the electronic age, like the librarian of the ancient and medieval worlds,

will have to be a scholar among scholars. He or she will be the information specialist in every research group, the person who helps the group keep up with and understand the state of knowledge and its history (and) the librarian will serve an international community of scholars in his or her field. The locations of librarian and colleagues will be designated by electronic addresses, not mail codes.[7]

Both Drucker and Chodorow asserted that after the new technologies are mature and integrated fully into the culture, the emphasis will return to content. This is the juncture where librarian–faculty collaboration finds its strength: when two or more educators combine talents and interests in the pursuit of the mutual goal of teaching students how to access, contextualize, evaluate, and synthesize information as a core part of their educational experience.

As the amount of information available escalates, knowledge of how information is organized and published, and the capacity to teach the skills needed to gain efficient access to it, will continue to be highly valued and will mark the role of the contemporary librarian in the era of collaborative enterprise.

As information increases in sheer volume, librarians working with scholars may need to be more focused on the literature of the field in one particular discipline. Librarian reference generalists or librarians attempting to keep current in "the social sciences" or "the physical sciences" will be challenged to function as collaborative partners with teaching faculty who are practicing within a niche of scholarship, such as a medieval scholar. As Chodorow suggested, the librarian who can participate as a colleague may be sought after by a community of scholars who gather together across institutional boundaries.

CONCLUSION
The future looks bright for librarians who embrace their emergent roles as teachers and scholars. In many ways, technology is a vehicle

for expanding the librarian's sphere of influence and complements the traditional values of our profession: service, quality, universal access, and cooperation. Collaboration with teaching and research faculty is certainly one of the key elements to our profession's future.

NOTES

1. Peter F. Drucker, "The Next Information Revolution," *Forbes* 162, no. 4 (Aug. 24, 1998): pS47 (7).

2. Sheila D. Creth, " The Electronic Library: Slouching toward the Future or Creating a New Information Environment," Follett Lecture Series, UKOLN, 1996 [cited 6 Aug. 1999]. Available from <http://www.ukoln.ac.uk/services/papers/follett/creth/paper.html> (6 Aug. 1999).

3. Abigail Loomis, "Building Coalitions for Information Literacy," in *Information Age: Redefining the Librarian,* comp. Fifteenth Annual Task Force of the Library Instruction Round Table of the ALA (Englewood, Colo.: Libraries Unlimited, 1995).

4. Ibid.

5. Stanley Chodorow, "The Medieval Future of Intellectual Culture: Scholars and Librarians in the Age of the Electron" (address to the ARL Membership Meeting, 1996 [cited 6 Aug. 1999]. Available from <http://www.arl.org/arl/proceedings/temp/129/chodorow.html>.)

6. Ibid.

7. Ibid.

Conclusion

This has been a long journey. It began simply as members of a university-wide committee and concludes with the publication of this book. Throughout the process, we have learned about the power of working together in a changing educational environment.

What did we learn? We know now that insight proceeds from listening, listening to the other as well to oneself. Listening is a dance of creation and re-creation. It increases the pulse of life all around us. I listen to you who listen to me who listens to you, and on and on. It is a listening that consciously eschews evaluation. Listening in this way required that we set aside our own constructions and stories about what is right, good, and appropriate, and plunge into a zone of uncertainty where we did not know. Open listening, we call it. It is a listening for surprise rather than for confirmation. In that listening, ideas flourish, insight unfolds.

We also learned that trust is the basis of authentic relationships. Trust is a gift, spontaneously given. We trusted each other to share what we felt strongly about, what we believed to be true, what we hoped for, what we were thinking, even if the thinking was not complete or completely formed. Trust was the river in which to move collaboration. Without trust, we could not have experienced the nurturing that work provides. Rather, we would have put up with, we believe, the usual suspicions, aggravations, and accusations about the other that mark so many attempts to work together. Without trust, the work would have been dry and bitter, and we might have felt ground up and angry, complaining to whomever would listen, eager to get it over with rather than lingering to delight in the flow of all the channels and gullies, the turns and unexpected surprises that work with another professional can offer.

Finally, what we learned from this collaboration was the power of dialogue. The listening we did was a forum in which ideas, conceptual relationships, interpretations, insights could bubble to the top of the flow of conversation. Serious conversation about what matters most to us encourages us to show up as ourselves. What greater gift can a human being receive than the summons to be fully alive in the moment? With that gift, new connections were born—connections that, we believe, would not have been possible in solitary endeavor. We wish you well as you embark on your collaborative journeys. We hope you experience as many surprises and joys as we have. Happy sailing!

Contributors

Susan Ariew is college librarian for education and human development at Virginia Tech University, in Blacksburg; e-mail address: saa@vt.edu.

Sarah Beasley is education/social science librarian at Portland State University Library, in Portland, Oregon; e-mail address: beasleys@pdx.edu.

Jean Caspers is outreach and instruction librarian at Oregon State University in Corvallis; e-mail address: jean.caspers@orst.edu.

Doug Cook is reference/media librarian at Shippensburg University, in Shippensburg, Pennsylvania; e-mail address: dlcook@ship.edu.

Bee Gallegos is education librarian at Arizona State University West, in Phoenix; e-mail address: bee.gallegos@asu.cdu.

Shellie Jeffries is education librarian at Wayne State University, in Detroit; e-mail address: ac0656@wayne.edu.

Katy Lenn is education librarian at the University of Oregon, in Eugene; e-mail address: klenn@oregon.uoregon.edu.

Dick Raspa is professor of interdisciplinary studies at Wayne State University in Detroit; e-mail address: aa2267@wayne.edu.

Mike Tillman is curriculum and juvenile materials librarian at California State University, in Fresno; e-mail address: michael_tillman@csufresno.edu.

Jennie Ver Steeg is education librarian at Northern Illinois University in Dekalb; e-mail address: jversteeg@niu.edu.

Scott Walter is information services librarian at the Education, Human Ecology, Psychology, and Social Work Library, Ohio State University, in Columbus; e-mail address: walter.123@osu.edu.

Dane Ward is coordinator of instruction services in the university library at Central Michigan University, in Mt. Pleasant; e-mail address: dane.ward@cmich.edu.

Thomas Wright is education librarian at Brigham Young University in Provo, Utah; e-mail address: Tom_Wright@BYU.EDU.